I0460132

ESCAPING
SOLACE

BOOK TWO OF A TRILOGY

SKYE BELLARMINE

Star Skye Press LLC

Escaping Solace
Skye Bellarmine

Published by Star Skye Press, LLC, St Charles, MO / Dallas, TX
Copyright ©2025 Skye Bellarmine
All rights reserved.

No part of this publication may be reproduced, stored in a retrieval system, or transmitted in any form or by any means, electronic, mechanical, photocopying, recording, scanning, or otherwise, except as permitted under Section 107 or 108 of the 1976 United States Copyright Act, without the prior written permission of the Publisher. Requests to the Publisher for permission should be addressed to Permissions Department, Star Skye Press, LLC, Skye@StarSkyePress.com

Limit of Liability/Disclaimer of Warranty: While the publisher and author have used their best efforts in preparing this book, they make no representations or warranties with respect to the accuracy or completeness of the contents of this book and specifically disclaim any implied warranties of merchantability or fitness for a particular purpose. No warranty may be created or extended by sales representatives or written sales materials. The advice and strategies contained herein may not be suitable for your situation. You should consult with a professional where appropriate. Neither the publisher nor author shall be liable for any loss of profit or any other commercial damages, including but not limited to special, incidental, consequential, or other damages.

This is a work of fiction. The story, all names, characters, and incidents portrayed in this literary work are fictitious. No identification with actual persons (living or deceased), places, buildings, and products is intended or should be inferred. Any similarity to actual persons, living or deceased, or actual events, is purely coincidental.

Project Management and Book Design: Davis Creative Publishing, LLC / DavisCreativePublishing.com
Cover Design: Missy Asikainen
Editor: Cheryl Roberts Oliver

Names: Bellarmine, Skye, author.
Title: Escaping solace : book two of a trilogy / Skye Bellarmine.
Description: St. Charles, MO ; Dallas, TX : Star Skye Press LLC, [2025]
Identifiers: ISBN: 979-8-9888398-3-5 (paperback) | 979-8-9888398-4-2 (ebook) | LCCN: 2025900311
Subjects: LCSH: Young women--Fiction. | Abused wives--Fiction. | Divorce--Fiction. | Man-woman relationships--Fiction. | Narcissism--Fiction. | Self-protective behavior--Fiction. | Passive- aggressive personality--Fiction. | BISAC: FICTION / Women. | FAMILY & RELATIONSHIPS / Abuse / General. | FAMILY & RELATIONSHIPS / Abuse / Domestic Partner Abuse.
Classification: LCC: PS3602.E45733 E83 2025 | DDC: 813/.6--dc23

2025

ATTENTION CORPORATIONS, UNIVERSITIES, COLLEGES AND PROFESSIONAL ORGANIZATIONS: Quantity discounts are available on bulk purchases of this book for educational, gift purposes, or as premiums for increasing magazine subscriptions or renewals. Special books or book excerpts can also be created to fit specific needs. For information, please contact Skye Bellarmine, Star Skye Press, LLC, Skye@StarSkyePress.com, BreakingSolaceBook.com, StarSkyePress.com

This book is an absolute page-turner, and I'm eager to dive into the trilogy's third installment! The author masterfully keeps readers emotionally invested from start to finish while offering a vivid and insightful portrayal of a narcissistic relationship. The storytelling is both gripping and relatable, making it hard to put down. I highly recommend this book to anyone seeking a powerful and thought-provoking read.

Madison Frederick
International Best-Selling Author of
Untangle the Web of Narcissism:
From Deceit and Chaos to Sanity

The second volume of the Solace *trilogy,* Escaping Solace, *left me both shaken and filled with hope. Skye Bellarmine delivers a poignant depiction of what it's like to be in a relationship with a partner suffering from narcissistic disorder. As the story of Tali and her husband, Blake Solace, unfolds, this book tugs at the heartstrings and keeps readers holding their breath for the epilogue. More than a compelling narrative, it serves as a powerful reminder of the importance of being present for our loved ones—and allowing their presence to support us through life's most challenging moments.*

Sophie Rouméas
sophieroumeas.com
Happy Author,
Transgenerational and Mindfulness Coach,
Hypnosis Practitioner

Dedication:

To all those reaching beyond the chaos...
keep up the good fight.

Prologue

The call ends. Tali Solace sits in silence. Sobbing, tears stream down her suntanned cheeks as thoughts ricochet off the walls of her mind. She struggles to catch her breath, reflecting on her conversation with her new attorney, Jay Richards. So many questions...so many decisions...and the big question... should she stay, or should she go?

Her therapist, Shannon, shared facts and insights about narcissism during a recent therapy session. Her words, "Narcissism isn't curable," continue to resonate in Tali's mind. She looks over at Jasper, the golden retriever pup lying on the rug in front of the hearth, while Misty, the gray kit, purrs from her perch on the windowsill. Tali stares out at the setting sun...the end of another day...possibly the end of a traumatic relationship.

She thinks about Jay's question. *He asked if I believed that Blake's and my marriage is irreparably broken...is it? I wonder...*

I can say that I may still love him...but I think that may be a stretch with his rages...gaslighting...manipulation. She cries uncontrollably. Jasper curls up next to her. She begins to drift off into another realm of consciousness as a wave of numbness courses through her body. *The journey is beginning.* She knows this leg of her life "journey" will be difficult. She sleepily tries to envision her escape route...so many questions. Will she ever find the answers?

1

She Sees the Lies

I t's Wednesday afternoon. Tali finishes work and goes home to take care of Jasper and Misty before heading to the restaurant to meet Bentley, Tali's best friend for many years, for dinner. Upon arriving at the Seaside Grill, Tali gives her key to the valet and walks into the restaurant. Bentley is waiting for her in the lobby, and he scoops her up in a huge hug, saying, "I've missed you!"

Tali starts to cry as she hugs him with all her strength, saying, "I've missed you too, babe!" They hold each other tightly for a moment as Tali's tears begin to subside, and then they stand apart to look at each other and laugh.

"Looking good, Tali, like you're getting back into college tennis team shape...but of course, you always look great!"

Tali blushes, "Aw, Bentley, thanks. You look buff, as ever. Tesca's keeping you in shape, even with your Wall Street office job. How was last week's half marathon? She posted your warm-up on TikTok...just like old college track team days...huh?"

Bentley laughs. "I'm still recovering from that event...she's a brutal trainer...why do you think I'm standing up waiting for you? My legs are still stiff. She's an amazing partner."

The maître d' appears and inquires whether they are ready to be seated. They nod and are led to a beachfront table with a spectacular view of the impending sunset. Bentley pulls out a chair for Tali and then seats himself. Once settled in, they both stare out at the surf beneath the setting sun for a moment, each collecting their thoughts.

Bentley is angry about Blake's traumatizing Tali, his best friend. He's also contemplating proposing to Tesca and wonders again what marriage is all about. He wants to talk with Tali about everything. Trying to decide where to begin, he puts that conversation on hold for another time. He knows Tali is totally consumed by her thoughts about Blake.

They both return to the present moment and smile as their gazes meet. Tali's eyes are filled with tearful speculation about what the future has in store for her, while Bentley's eyes depict a compassionate glimmer of hope for Tali.

Intrigued by his expression, Tali says, "So dude, I'm so grateful you're here. I really need a healthy dose of you."

He responds as he reaches for her hands, "Of course, Turt," using the nickname he gave her in college. "I'm always here for you, you know that." He smiles his big, intoxicating smile.

She returns his smile and says, "I'm scared about seeing Blake when he gets back tomorrow. I should confront him about lying to me about his 'business' trip and his meeting with you. I'm ready to stand up to him...actually, no, I'm not. Or am I!" She looks at Bentley with questioning eyes.

He replies, "Babe, you're strong and way more emotionally intelligent than Blake. Let's rehearse what you are going to say to him when he arrives. And, after you talk with him, you have plans to go to Molly's house with the pets, yes? I don't want you staying at the townhouse alone with Blake."

She says, "That's the plan. So many ideas about what to say to him are swirling around in my mind right now. And, yes, Molly and Chad know that I'll be coming over tomorrow evening. Molly's going to pick up the pets tomorrow before Blake arrives."

"Great! Now," Bentley smiles, "let's look at the menu and order an amazing dinner...a nice wine...and catch up. I've missed you!" They enjoy a delicious dinner and conversation filled with joking, laughing, bantering...just two besties hanging out together. After coffee, Bentley pays the check, and they go for a walk on the beach to talk about what Tali should say to Blake during tomorrow's confrontation. Then, they go their separate ways.

Tali pulls into her garage and enters the townhouse at 11:00 p.m. Jasper greets her excitedly while Misty yawns and purrs from the windowsill in the hearth room. She's still wide awake, anxious thoughts swirling about tomorrow's confrontation with Blake, so she grabs Jasper's leash and heads to the beach.

The following day, Tali awakens at 5:30 a.m. She sits on the side of the bed for a few minutes. Since the car wreck, she mentally prepares herself for the first steps of each day, knowing there will be some initial pain and stiffness. It's okay. She reminds herself that at least she learned how to walk again. It was touch and go for a while. It took a lot of time and determination for her to recover from the head-on collision with a wrong-way driver. It was questionable whether she would ever walk or be able to do her design work again. She's thankful for the blessings in her life, for God's grace and mercy.

After a few moments, she stands up and walks to the kitchen. Jasper stirs a bit but doesn't leave her spot at the end of the bed. Misty doesn't even move. Tali gets a glass of ice water while she waits for the Keurig to brew a cup of Starbuck's French Roast. Blake is due back in Newport Beach today from his "business trip" to New York. She wishes he would fly straight to his place. He insisted he come here, saying he missed her and wanted to check on her before returning to work in Monterey.

That's a crock of lies, she thinks to herself. *He wants to see if I know where he's been and what he's been up to. Of course I do, but how do I let him know that I know he's been trying to sabotage me with my clients and gaslighting me to friends and neighbors? Who does Blake think he is?* She feels her anger rising. Jasper senses this and runs over to her, tail wagging for hugs and pets. Tali reaches down to pet Jasper and then grabs her cup of coffee and Jasper's leash to go for a walk on the beach before work. She texts Bentley. He's out jogging. He replies that he'll catch up with them at Tia's. About thirty minutes later, Tali, Bentley, and Jasper meet at Tia's Beach Café for water and smoothies.

"Good morning, Tali and Jasper," says Tia, the café owner, as she greets them with a smile and hugs. Tia loves Jasper and has her bowl ready with ice water when they arrive.

Tali greets Tia with a smile and a hug.

"Who's this handsome guy with you today?" She smiles and winks at Tali.

Smiling, Tali responds, "This is Bentley. We've been best friends forever. He's visiting here this week. Can we get a table near the water?"

"Sure," says Tia. She picks up Jasper's water bowl and leads them all to their table. On numerous occasions, Tia witnessed Blake scolding Tali while walking past her café. She just wants Tali to be happy. She thinks, *Thank goodness Tali has Jasper to go on walks with...and her good friend Molly...and now I'm glad to know that she has a supportive male friend in her tribe. I want her to be happy.* Tia sighs.

Bentley and Tali joke and share a few laughs while enjoying their smoothies and avocado toast. Jasper happily laps water and chews on ice cubes and dog treats Tia has given her.

"Let's make a plan," Bentley suggests.

"Agreed," Tali nods. They decide Tali will text Bentley when Blake arrives at her place and go from there.

After breakfast, Tali and Jasper return to the townhouse, and Bentley goes to his hotel. Because Blake is returning, Tali has arranged to work from home today. She intends to confront him about his lies and whereabouts.

After filling the pets' water and food bowls, she goes upstairs to shower and prepare for the day. She has a 9:00 a.m. Zoom meeting with the yacht club commander, Gordon Silvers. "Ironic," she says out loud, "meeting with Gordon before I engage in conversation with Blake this afternoon. Two men, different vocations and life experiences, yet basically the same DNA...the same controlling personalities."

Tali is in her art studio/office at 8:55 a.m. and logs into Zoom. Gordon logs in at 9:01 a.m. The meeting starts with Gordon complaining about the traffic on the way to the yacht club this morning.

Tali remains quietly composed until he finishes, and begins with a pleasant, "Hello, Mr. Silvers. Let's start with design changes based on your requests..." The conversation ensues.

At 10:25 a.m. sharp, Gordon says, "I need to go. I have another very important meeting here at the club in five minutes. Thanks for the changes. Send me the drafts, and I'll review them when I have time this weekend. I'll probably have more changes. You're making progress toward the new look I want for this establishment. Call my admin to schedule a time for you to come out here next week." He logs off.

"Oh man," she says quietly. "That was quite the meeting... just warming up for this evening with Blake." She looks at Jasper and Misty, both snoozing, enjoying the warm breeze gently wafting through the open windows.

2

The Confrontation

Blake's flight arrives in Newport Beach at 4:00 p.m. When his plane lands, he texts Tali. "Where would you like to go for dinner?"

She replies, "The place on Grand that opened last month—the Nautilus. I've heard great things about the menu."

He texts back, "Sure, babe. How about you call for reservations? I should be home in about an hour, depending on traffic. Xoxo"

Tali calls the restaurant and makes reservations, then packs a duffle and bags for Jasper and Misty. While packing, she calls Bentley and shares the evening plan with him. He'll be near the Nautilus when she and Blake arrive, and he will be available while Tali talks with Blake over dinner. They agree that Tali confronting Blake about his lies and behaviors at a restaurant will be better than her being alone with him in the townhouse.

Molly comes over to pick up the pets and the bags before Blake gets home from the airport. Molly and Tali talk for a few minutes, and Molly encourages Tali and affirms that she is doing the right thing in confronting Blake this evening. "It's time," she says.

Tali hugs her and says, "I know, but it's still hard."

Molly agrees and squeezes her tighter. Molly and the pets leave, and Tali walks back into the townhouse. She sits in the hearth room in prayerful silence, seeking direction, strength, and solitude. Ten minutes later, she hears the garage door go up and Blake's voice. He's on the phone bragging to his brother Thomas about his business trip to NYC and how great he was in all the meetings. As he walks into the kitchen, he waves to Tali and lets out his shallow little laugh at something Thomas said.

It's probably something mean about someone. Tali thinks.

He ends the call and walks over to Tali to kiss and hug her. She bristles a bit, but not enough to cause Blake to think something is up. He says, "Hi babe, where's the pet gang?"

"They're at Molly and Chad's place playing for the evening. Thought you and I could use some time to catch up."

"Oh, okay...I guess," says Blake. "So, are you ready to go out? What time is our reservation?"

"7:00 p.m.," says Tali. "Thought you might want some time to wind down here before we drive to the restaurant. Let's leave in thirty minutes."

"Sure thing," says Blake. I'll change...the Nautilus is business casual, yes?"

"Yes," says Tali.

"Cool," says Blake. Twenty minutes later, he returns to the hearth room wearing the new sports shirt and blazer he bought in NYC. "What do you think of my new outfit?" he asks as he spins around.

Tali notices that he reeks of a new cologne. She smiles and says, "Nice."

"And..." he inquires as he walks over to her, "My new scent. It's the latest in NYC men's fashionable fragrances. What do you think?"

"Um...interesting...didn't you wear something similar in college?"

"Kinda...not really...this one's way more expensive than that one, and it smells much better! I love the way I smell! Okay, let's go. You ready?"

"Sure," says Tali. They walk into the garage. "Let's take my car."

When they arrive at the Nautilus, the valet walks up to them to park their car. Blake sneers and motions the valet away.

"Let's keep it easy," Tali says, giving the valet the car keys.

Blake's annoyed at her contradiction, but exits the car. The valet hands Tali the valet retrieval ticket, and they walk to the restaurant hostess stand. She acknowledges their reservation and leads them to a beachfront table for two. After being seated, Blake looks at Tali and says, "I missed you, beautiful. You look good."

It's only been a few days, she thinks. "Let's order starters, and then we need to talk."

Blake looks a bit irritated that she didn't immediately love his compliment. He wonders what's up, and what she knows.

After the two Sauvignon Blancs arrive, Tali proposes a toast: "Time to figure out our lives."

As the two glasses clink and Blake sips, he asks, "What do you mean?"

Unable to hide her feelings any longer, she asks, "Where were you on your trip? You told me you were going on a business trip. I called your office and was told you were taking personal days and that they didn't know where you were going. Of course, Bentley called me to tell me you were in NYC trying to bad-mouth me to my friends. By the way, I know you snooped in my art room office and tried to hurt my client relationships. What do you have to say for yourself? I'm calling you out...right here...right now."

"Babe, I've been concerned about you and your emotional state lately. You seem stressed and unsure about your new clients and obligations. I'm trying to help you be your best. Please don't get me wrong. I love you. I want the best for you. The best for us. I went to NYC to talk face-to-face with Bentley so that I could help you. As for you thinking I was snooping in your art room and talking with your clients behind your back, that's ludicrous. You're delusional. Don't blame me for you being disorganized with your client files."

Tali is silent, thinking, *I didn't say anything about the files being out of order. He just admitted something.* She says, "You are lying. You tried to sabotage me professionally and flew to NYC to bad-mouth me to my best friend. I don't know you anymore. I'm done, Blake." Tali stands up and starts to walk out of the restaurant.

Blake quickly stands and blocks her path. His eyes are blackening as his face reddens. He reaches for her arm and says under his breath, "Don't make a scene, Tali. You always say that potential design clients are everywhere. Wouldn't want to make a scene here, now, would we?" He forces her to come with him onto the restaurant terrace.

She's trying to hold back the tears and stand up to him.

"You're not leaving." He looks around to see if anyone is staring at them. "We're going back into the restaurant and resuming our dinner. I'm deeply concerned about your mental problems. You're not strong enough to do anything on your own. You need me. You know that. Let's turn around and walk calmly back to our table."

She pulls her arm out of his grasp and walks back into the restaurant.

As they reseat themselves at the table, the server asks, "Is everything okay?"

Tali begins to speak. Blake cuts her off, "Everything's fine. My wife here just needed some fresh air. I think we're ready to order." They order appetizers and dinner.

After the server walks away, Tali says, "Actually, I've been thinking about us," she says. He looks up at her with eyebrows raised.

"And? What conclusions have you come to?"

"I'm not sure, Blake. Things are not right between us. They haven't been for a long time. I don't know what to do. Maybe we need some time apart to sort through some stuff."

Blake replies, "I disagree. We must stay together to work through whatever you imagine is going on with us." He forces a smile as he reaches across the table to hold her hand.

Tali retracts her hand and looks him squarely in the eyes. "Blake, you don't seem to understand what I'm saying. You have hurt me in so many ways."

"Tali, you're delusional." Blake's voice escalates. "We need to get you some help."

Tali stands and walks quickly out of the restaurant, drawing concerned looks from patrons and staff. She always keeps a spare key fob with her and reaches for the key as she heads for the valet lot. She spots her car and runs toward it.

Blake is right behind her. He grabs her from behind and places his hands around her waist. She feels her body tighten. He jerks one of her arms behind her back and pushes her face-first into the driver's side window. "Now," he screams, "what lies were you spouting about me trying to sabotage your career? Those are damn lies. You're so delusional that you're now making stuff up to make me look bad." His voice turns to a sinister whisper, "You know damn well that I'm smarter than you. You'll never make me look like the bad guy in our so-called marriage. Mom was right about you. You're an airhead. I could've done so much better."

Tali's head is pressed hard against the car. The action stirs her memory of the night she woke up bleeding in the bathroom. She remembers Blake pushing her into the towel rack and leaving her on the bathroom floor with her head bleeding. The memory of that night is terrifying. She tries to turn her head and wriggle out of Blake's grasp. Tears are streaming down her face. Between sobs, she pleads, "Let go of me. You're hurting me. We can talk about this."

He tightens his grip while grumbling in guttural tones.

With her free hand, Tali still fumbles with the key fob to open the driver's door. She squirms and drops her purse while trying to escape his grasp. She recalls some self-defense moves that her trainer taught her. She kicks her good leg, the one without the metal plates, up and back, landing her hamstring in Blake's crotch with just enough force to cause him to release his grip on her.

He grimaces as he falls to the ground, "What the hell!"

She opens the car door, grabs her purse off the ground, jumps in and drives away as quickly as possible. She heads down the street away from the restaurant, crying uncontrollably. When she's out of sight of the restaurant, she pulls into a well-lit gas station parking lot so that if Blake figures out a way to follow her, she won't be alone. She calls Bentley. Since leaving the restaurant, her phone has been buzzing with calls from Blake. She connects with Bentley but can't talk.

"What's going on?" Bentley asks. "Is he with you? Are you okay?"

She takes some deep breaths to try to calm down enough to talk.

Bentley says, "Tali, talk to me."

Finally able to speak, she says in broken syllables, "He hurt me. I left. In the car." She continues to sob.

"Okay. Where are you? I'm coming to get you."

She looks around her. She took a left turn out of the parking lot. She collects her thoughts for a few seconds and pulls up the GPS on her phone. It gives her location, and she screenshots the map app pic and sends it to Bentley.

He says, "Just hold tight. Don't go anywhere. I'll be there in four minutes."

Tali says, "Thanks. I'm scared."

"I know, Turt. I'm on my way."

Tali sits in her car with the doors locked.

Meanwhile, back at the Nautilus, Blake was unable to chase after Tali due to his injured crotch and the fact that he didn't have a car. Staggering, he stumbles into the restaurant. The maître d' and their server hand him the bill just as a police car pulls up outside the restaurant.

As the policeman walks inside, Blake curses under his breath. He doubles over and holds his crotch. As the policeman and maître d' approach, he says quickly, "Officer, nothing is going on here. I'm fine. My wife attacked me, and then she drove off. I can give you a few addresses of where she might be so that you can arrest her for assaulting…"

The officer cuts him off. "Sir, I was called to help a woman who was being attacked in this parking lot. The maître d' told me about you chasing a woman out of the restaurant and then pushing her up against a car. Is that true?"

Blake looks away, then focuses his darkened eyes on the officer. "Officer, that's my wife. She was having a panic attack. I was trying to embrace her to calm her down. The doctor told me to try to hold her when she has a mental episode. That's all I was trying to do here. It's all a big misunderstanding." He looks over at the maître d', who has a doubtful expression.

The maître d' says, "I was only trying to ensure everyone was okay. All I know is what I saw."

Blake says, "You misinterpreted what you saw."

The police officer is taking notes. He then says, "I need to see your driver's license."

Blake says, "Of course, officer."

The officer walks back to his car to scan Blake's license. He comes back and hands the license to Blake. "I've recorded this evening's call in my log. I hope you find your wife and that she's okay."

Blake says, "Thank you, officer." Then, he walks into the restaurant to order a double bourbon on the rocks and pay the bill. "What a night," he texts his brother, Thomas. "Tali was worse than I've ever seen her. She is mental. I wish I had some of your military training. She kicked me in the nuts."

It is nearly 10 p.m. when he dials Molly's number.

Molly answers sleepily, "Hello? Blake?" Normally, Molly would not answer such a late call, but she is concerned about Tali.

"Hey, is Tali there?"

Molly hesitates and replies, "No, she's not. What's going on, Blake? Where is she?"

"We argued, and she stormed out of the restaurant. I thought she might have gone to your place."

"No, she's not here," Molly says. "I'll call the police and..."

Before finishing her sentence, Blake says, "Oh no, don't do that. That would just upset her more. I'll look for her and try to calm her down. She was in such an emotional, almost frantic state when she left. She's not mentally well. I hope she doesn't do something drastic, like hurting herself. I worry about her." He pauses for Molly's response.

As he talked, Molly texted Tali, who replied she was okay. Molly says to Blake, "Tali's fine. I just got a text from her. You can go back to the townhouse. Bye." She ends the call.

Blake, seething with anger and still in pain from Tali's kick to his crotch, stays at the bar nursing his second drink. Around midnight, he calls a taxi. When he arrives at the townhouse, he calls Thomas.

"What's up, little brother?" Thomas asks.

"OMG! Tali said she wants time to figure out *her* life. Not our 'life.' She ran out of the restaurant! I don't know what happened. She's crazy, man, just plain crazy."

"Wow, dude," Thomas says. "I'm sorry. Are you okay?"

"No. I'm not okay. My wife is mental. My new job is not going great. I don't know where my wife is at the moment. I have to fly back to Monterey tomorrow...actually, it's after midnight... so make that today. So, no, things are not okay. Tali's totally off the rails. She's liable to do something crazy, like tell people that I hurt her. She thinks I'm trying to sabotage her career. I tell you, man, she's nuts."

"Just calm down, Blake. We can figure this out. You know I'll do whatever you need me to do. Maybe you should call the police to help find her since you think she's out of her mind."

Blake says, "No, they wouldn't care. I took a taxi back to the townhouse after she drove off in the car about two hours ago. I've been calling and texting her. No response. I'll wait to see if she comes home before I drive to the airport later this morning."

"Okay. Sounds good, bro. Let me know if you need anything. I'm happy to help you manage your crazy wife. She has no right to hurt you."

"Sure thing. Thanks." Blake ends the call. It may have been the two double bourbons or the pain in his crotch, but Blake's thoughts suddenly started to turn against him, like maybe it was his fault and not Tali's. He worried that he'd pushed her too hard against the car. Questioning himself, he hears the voice in his head. *Don't be stupid. It's all on her. She's a mess. It's good you scared her. She needs to know who's in control and that any failure is all her fault.* He felt better after his internal pep talk and was soon sound asleep.

3

Just the Facts

Tali waits in her car, still parked in a well-lit area of the twenty-four-hour gas station. Bentley drives up and parks next to her car. She unlocks the doors, and he quickly slides into the passenger seat. She's crying and shaking.

He puts his arms around her and tries to calm her, asking, "What happened?"

Still sobbing, she tries to catch her breath. "He attacked me! He pinned me up against the car at the restaurant and threatened me! I remembered the attack in the bathroom, the one where he claimed I fell. I didn't fall. He hit me and left me there, bleeding on the floor."

"OMG. What happened tonight? Are you hurt?"

"He smashed my face against the car. I kicked him in the crotch and drove away, then I called you." She looks up and hugs him. "I'm so grateful you are here."

"Of course," he says as he hugs her tighter. "Okay, let's talk this through. Does Molly know what happened?"

"Yes, I texted her. She has the pets. I'll stay at her place tonight."

"Good," says Bentley, adding, "Call your boss, Sydney in the morning and tell her you'll spend a long weekend in Huntington Beach with me and my family. Tell her what Blake did to you. She'll understand why you need to get away for a few days. I'll check out of my hotel and pick you up at 10:00 a.m. We'll get brunch on the way to my parents' house. Can Molly take care of Jasper and Misty over the long weekend?"

"Yes, she can. She's already offered."

With a quiet voice, Bentley adds, "Tali, I'm not demanding that you come with me to my parents' house. Please know that. I'm offering some time away with a family who loves you. Please know I'm not trying to control you in any way."

She smiles. "You're my best friend. I know you're trying to help me." She hugs him. "I'd better get over to Molly's place. She has work in the morning, and I know she's waiting up for me. I'll see you at 10:00 a.m." She looks into his eyes, crying again, whispering, "Thank you so much."

He says, "I'm here for you, Turt, always. You know that. I'll follow you to Molly's and then drive back to my hotel." He squeezes her hands as he exits her car.

4

Lost Memories Returned and New Ones Made

Tali awakens the following day in Molly's guest room. Jasper and Misty are sleeping nearby. She goes to the kitchen, makes a cup of coffee, and walks outside to the pool, settling into a chaise with her coffee and journal. She writes.

Dear Josie...It's Friday. Confronting Blake last night was scary. I'm so glad we were in a public place. He attacked me in the parking lot. It made me remember that night in the bathroom when he hurt me, lied to me, left me alone. It's over. I'm going to complete the documents that Jay Richards sent me. Maybe Bentley can help me with them while hanging out with his family. I can only hope. I'm so blessed to have friends like Bentley and Molly and a boss like Sydney. I'll call Mamita after I let Sydney know I'm

*staying with Bentley's family for a few days. Thanks for
being my safe space, Josie.*

After Molly heads to work, Tali calls Sydney to share details
about her encounter with Blake and request time off. Sydney
reassures Tali that she can take whatever time she needs. Tali
is grateful to be blessed with such an awesome mentor and
friend. Then, she calls Mamita to talk while she gets ready to
meet Bentley. Mamita comforts her daughter and offers to visit
when Tali returns from spending the weekend with Bentley's
family. Tali loves the idea.

Bentley picks up Tali, and they stop at Tia's Beach Café for
brunch before driving to Huntington Beach. They stayed with
small talk, clearly avoiding the desperation Tali was feeling
after Blake's rough treatment last night. Arriving at Bentley's
family home, they drive around to the back and see his mom
working in her garden while his dad sits at a glass table on the
back patio with his computer. Bentley's mom, Candace, is a flo-
rist, and his dad, Ben, is an IP attorney. His parents waved and
motioned for them to park near the pool house by the eucalyp-
tus tree. Bentley parks the car and opens the passenger door for
Tali, who is already smiling and squealing with delight as she
receives hugs from Candace and Ben.

"So good to see you, Tali!" his parents exclaim together.

Tali replies, "Thanks so much for inviting me! I'm
excited to hang out with you two and your son for a few days!"

"Of course," says Candace, as she puts her arm around Tali
and walks to the patio. Ben and Bentley get the bags out of the
car and bring them inside—Bentley's to his room and Tali's to
the poolside guest room. The guys are chatting and joking as
they deliver the luggage. Then, they walk out to the patio to join

Candace and Tali. Candace pours some fresh limeade while Ben slices a fresh pineapple and honeydew melon.

Bentley leans back in his chair and breathes deeply. "Wow, I've missed you guys...and this ocean breeze...it's just 'So Cal life.' Man..." His voice trails off as he gazes out at the pool with the surf beyond."

Candace reaches for his hand and says, "We've missed you too, son. We're so proud of you and the work you're doing in NYC! How much longer before you plan to bring your venture capital project to CA?"

"Thanks, Mom. Probably within the next year. My team and I have made significant progress with recent investment strategies and connections with potential investors who want to partner with us. I'm ready. Tesca has been talking with associates on the West Coast about transitioning to a law firm here."

Ben comments, "You know I'll do whatever I can to help her find the firm she's seeking."

"We both appreciate that, Dad," Bentley says. "Okay, enough about me. We have a beautiful guest who is moving and shaking the interior design world. And not only in Newport Beach. Someone's been invited to lead a project in Paris...hmm?"

"Tali...do tell!" says Candace.

"Bentley exaggerates...I'm developing some designs for a new client, and she says that if the Newport Beach project goes well, I might be invited to work on a project in Paris...not 'lead,' but be on the team."

Bentley smiles and says, "Tali's always humble." Looking at her, he says, "Turt, you're awesome."

She smiles as she blushes.

Candace says, "Sounds like a great opportunity, Tali." Ben agrees. The conversation continues with Tali complimenting

Candace on her beautiful garden with its bold colors. The ladies get up to tour the garden. Bentley and his dad go for a walk on the beach.

"I'm thinking about proposing to Tesca," Bentley announces to his father.

"My advice," his dad offers, "follow your heart."

Bentley expresses his concerns about Tali and her safety around Blake while sharing details on what's gone down the past few days.

His dad assures him, "We can help Tali with whatever she needs during the divorce battle."

"Thanks, Dad. I wish I could be here to help her, but I have to fly back to NYC on Tuesday. I'm happy to have time with you, Mom, and Tali this weekend. She's strong but needs our support to heal and get a fresh perspective as she files for divorce. What a journey she's embarking upon. I have friends in NYC who have traveled the divorce road with a narcissist. It's hard. I want to help Tali prepare for the fight. She has a good therapist, loving parents, strong friends, and, from what I hear, the best family law attorney in southern California, Jay Richards. She'll be fine. We just all need to help her through this experience."

"Wow, son," Ben says, "I'm so proud of you for being Tali's friend and supporting her. You two have always had each other's backs. Know that your mom and I are here for you and Tali...anything she needs. And, yes, I know of Jay Richards. His excellent reputation in family law goes far beyond southern California. Tali is in good hands."

"That's cool. I think she needs us to assist her in preparing some financial documents for the attorney while she's here." Bentley says.

"Sure thing. We should probably head back to the house. Your mom has prepared some of your favorite recipes for a casual lunch by the pool. Then we can all go for a swim if you and Tali would like."

"Awesome, Dad," Bentley says, putting his arm around his dad's shoulder. They walk side-by-side back to the house.

* * * * *

Blake wakes up with a hangover, but has to drive back to Monterey to get to work. He's been on the phone with his brother Thomas and has tried to reach Tali's friends, none of whom are answering. Blake's angry about what Tali said about him being manipulative, controlling, and a liar, knowing he's none of those things. He is concerned, though, that she has remembered that night he attacked her in the bathroom. Then he hears the voice in his head. *You're the one in charge. Don't feel sorry about being strong. If Tali weren't so weak and helpless, you wouldn't have to hurt her. You know what your mother would tell you.*

* * * * *

Over the weekend, Bentley and his dad assisted Tali with two documents that Jay Richards needed to begin the divorce filing process: the Statement of Position and the Statement of Income and Expenses.

Tali's phone pings with Blake's crickets ringtone all weekend as Blake calls her numerous times. She finally blocks Blake's number to have peace and refocus her mind on the documents. She'd been initiating conversations with Blake about their finances since she overheard him talking with his brother about some investment deals. She heard him say, "Tali would never understand the risk, but hopefully, there will be a high return." Since then, she's been researching investments and talking with Blake about their portfolio, taking copious notes during their discussions, which were monologues with Blake pontificating on how much he knows about financial instruments and how dense she is.

She'd been listening closely to Blake and seeing him differently lately. She has a pretty good grasp of their assets and financial obligations. With Bentley's and Ben's help, she put together a reasonable representation of their marital assets, liabilities, income, and expenses. They wrapped up those discussions on Saturday evening after dinner. On Sunday, Tali enjoyed time together with Bentley's family, hanging out with neighbors... swimming...laughing...being light-hearted. It was just what Tali needed.

Later that night, she did FaceTime with Molly to check on the pets. Molly assured her that all was well and inquired, "How are you?"

Tali hesitates, takes a deep breath, and replies, "I think I'm Okay. My cheek, neck, and wrist are bruised from Blake twisting my wrist behind my back and shoving me up against the car on Thursday night. Bentley's family is so sweet and loving to let me stay here this weekend. Bentley and his dad helped me put together the financial documents that Jay needs so I can file for divorce. OMG, Molly...this is a lot!"

"I know, my dear," Molly says softly. "We're all here to help you. We love you."

"Thank you!" Tali says with tears beginning to fall.

Molly says, "You're going to be fine. You have a tribe, Tali. You know that, right?"

Tali laughs softly and says, "I know. You're right. I love you."

"I love you, too. Now, get some rest. You're there through tomorrow, yes?"

"Yes," says Tali.

"Good. Enjoy. I'll see you on Tuesday when you get home."

"Okay. Cool. Thanks again for taking care of Jasper and Misty. You're the best! See you Tuesday!"

Tali opens her journal...

Dear Josie...I'm so thankful for my friends. I couldn't make it through this horrific experience by myself. My therapist advised me not to think about what ifs...if I hadn't married Blake and how I could have made such a mistake. It's hard not to question my decision to be with him. How did I miss all of those narcissistic red flags? The love bombing... gaslighting...manipulation...control...lies...hoovering... attempts to sabotage my career...even early on when he tried to forbid me from taking the internship in college at the firm where I now work? What was I thinking? How did I fall in love with this monster?

Tali weeps quietly as she writes, not wanting to wake anyone in the house. She closes her journal, extinguishes the light, and closes her eyes, but her mind is churning with many thoughts and memories. She fears what Blake will do when he's served with divorce papers. After a restless sleep, she wakes up to sunshine streaming through the window and the smell of bacon wafting through the house.

"Good morning," Tali says sleepily as she enters the kitchen. Candace is cutting fresh flowers for the table while Bentley prepares fresh fruit. Ben has already left for work, with plans to be home early that evening for dinner.

Candace walks over to Tali and hugs her. "Good morning, beautiful girl! How was your rest?"

"It was good, and thank you again for inviting me to stay here. I'm feeling a little more like myself today."

"That's good to hear, my dear," Candace says.

Bentley washes the fruit pulp off his hands and squeezes Tali, saying, "I have a surprise for you today!" He hesitates while Tali looks at him with anticipation.

"Okay, what do you have up your sleeve this time? Those 'surprises' in college...a little off the wall at times, dude...not bungee jumping again...I can't do that today..."

"No, no,...nothing like that," he says. "I got a text late last night from Noah and Jenna!" They're both in town for an IT conference. They arrived late last night and want to meet for dinner this evening!"

"OMG!" Tali squeals. "I haven't seen them since we all went on that trip right after graduation. Where are they living now?"

Bentley replies, "Jenna lives in Seattle, and Noah lives in Charlotte. They're in the IT field and both attending the same conference. Jenna also says she has some venture capitalist clients looking to invest in West Coast IT projects. She wants to discuss the programs my team and I are designing. No coincidences, right?"

"Wow," says Tali. "The four of us were quite the crew in college...so many laughs. We were always there for each other. Even the professors were interested in our latest stories and quips. So many memories! You're right...no coincidences. I could use some 'back-in-the-day' stories and friend time right now."

Candace adds, "Let's have your friends over for dinner this evening. It will be easier than you four trying to catch up in a noisy restaurant, and the kitchen never closes here." She smiles.

Bentley hugs his mom and says, "Thanks, Mom, you're the best."

Tali walks over to hug Candace and says, "Thanks so much. This will be fun! May I help you cook?"

Candace says, "Sure, that would be great! How about you and Bentley put together a menu while I run to the flower shop this morning. ? I have some orders to arrange. You two can hang out. Want to do lunch and go to the market at around 12:30 today?"

"Sounds like a plan," Tali says. The three of them enjoy an excellent breakfast before Candace leaves for work. Tali and Bentley clean the kitchen and store the leftovers before deciding on the menu for tonight's dinner gathering.

Tali is thinking, *How did I ever deserve a friend like Bentley? God is definitely carrying me through this life...I'm so thankful.* Tears begin to form in her blue eyes.

Bentley looks over at Tali as he sips his coffee. "What's wrong? Are you crying? Did I say something?"

"No," she says. "These are tears of joy. I'm happy right now. It's been a while since I've felt real happiness. Thanks for being my friend."

He squeezes her hand and says, "Of course I'm here for you. You've always been there for me, Turt."

They smile and return to menu planning and writing the grocery list.

Candace meets Tali and Bentley for lunch at a beachside restaurant, and then they go grocery shopping. Back home, Tali and Bentley bring in the groceries, and the three of them begin the meal prep. Ben arrives home from work around 4:30 p.m. He smiles as he walks into the kitchen filled with amazing smells...loads of laughter...and smiles all around. He kisses Candace and then goes upstairs to change.

When he returns to the kitchen, he and Bentley walk outside to the patio to start the grill and talk about their day.

"I'm working with a new IP client," Ben offers, "I can't share details because of an attorney-client fiduciary agreement, but I can tell you I'm excited about the project."

Bentley is happy that his dad loves his work. He hopes to bring that same enthusiasm and expertise to his career.

Jenna and Noah arrive at 5:00 p.m. They talk about old times, reliving great adventures. Laughter fills the evening air. Candace and Ben are thoroughly entertained.

5

Coast to Coast

After an early breakfast Tuesday morning, Bentley and Tali say goodbye to Candace and Ben. Bentley takes Tali home, then goes to the airport to catch his flight back to NYC.

Tali is thoughtful, happily reliving the weekend as she drives to Molly's to pick up the pets. Molly arranged to work remotely today since she knew Tali would stop by. Tali pulls into Molly's driveway and walks into the house through the open garage door just as Jasper runs up with pup rubs and slobbery kisses. She bends down to pet Jasper, and Misty wanders over, rubbing against her leg.

"What a precious greeting!"

"It's been quite a happy little zoo around here the past few days," Molly says, smiling. "Jasper loves the pool. Misty loves the lanai. My two just run around taunting the others all day. There were some intense games of tug of war with the rope toy. Jasper actually backed into the pool during one of those playtimes. She handled the klutzy moment quite gracefully, though, I must admit."

"Aww, thanks, Molly! You and Chad are so awesome to put up my littles while I was gone," Tali says as she hugs Molly. "Here are some fresh flowers that Bentley's mom sent for you. She's quite the horticulturist. Her gardens remind me of Monet's...just gorgeous and awe-inspiring."

"Thanks! These are beautiful!" Molly puts the flowers in a vase on the breakfast table. "I've been worried," she says.

Tali replies, "Me, too. It was so good to get away for a few days to redirect my thoughts and get ready to send the divorce papers to Blake."

"Wow...when will he be served?" Molly asks.

Tali replies, "Well, with Bentley and his dad's help putting the financial statements together, Jay thinks we'll be ready to send the divorce petition on Friday."

"This coming Friday?" Molly asks. "So soon?"

"Yes," says Tali. "Why wait? Blake attacked me multiple times...screamed at me daily...tried to sabotage my career, lied about me to my friends...lied about his supposed business trip... tried to make me doubt my decisions...and always questioned my sanity. That's too much to continue dealing with. I know Blake's mom is controlling. He always said that he didn't want to be like her. And his dad's so beaten down by his mom's abuse that they don't even try to communicate. I thought I could help Blake be the strong, yet not controlling, man he wanted to be. We talked a lot about that before we were married. I guess I missed the red flags. Blake will never change. Narcissists don't change. When a narcissist is abusing you, you have to get away."

"Sounds like you and your therapist have had some pretty thought-provoking therapy sessions. I'm so pleased you and

Shannon connected. That's awesome. It also sounds like Jay is expertly and expediently helping you through the divorce process. That is so good to hear, Tali. I'll say it again. Your tribe is here for you. You know that."

"Yes. I feel it. Thanks so much for connecting me with Shannon and Jay. You're so awesome!"

"You're welcome, my friend," Molly says and leans in to hug Tali. Molly helps Tali gather the pets' toys and blankets and gets everyone into Tali's car to drive home.

6

Blake Hoovers

Tali takes Jasper and Misty to the townhouse and then drives to her office. She's thinking about her lunchtime workout with her trainer, Ryan. It'll be a tough one. It's been a few weeks since she hit the gym. She'll share the recent self-defense tactic that potentially saved her from being further injured by Blake in the parking lot last week. Her mind wanders back to that night, and once again, she wonders how the marriage ever got this bad. She has a session with Shannon scheduled for to-morrow before Mamita arrives. She needs to get her life togeth-er...having a schedule with workouts and meetings will help. She hopes.

She parks her car on the deck and takes the stairs to her of-fice floor. The staff greets her warmly as she enters the office. She puts her briefcase and purse away and then walks down the hall to Sydney's office. She knocks. Sydney turns around and smiles from her drafting table. She asks Tali to close the door. The two ladies sit in Sydney's wing-back chairs to talk.

Sydney says, "How are you?"

Tali replies, "I don't know. I could say I'm fine, but I'm not. Blake assaulted me again. My memory returned about what happened 'that night' after we had dinner with Wren and Jess. He assaulted me that night, also. I'm done with him. Bentley and his dad helped me with the financial documents that my attorney needed. Thank you for letting me take some time off to deal with Blake. I needed to get away at Bentley's family home to put things in perspective. And thanks for letting me meet with our finance guy to review some investment details before I send the financial documents to my attorney today. You are the best boss! Mamita is arriving tomorrow after my lunch-time session with Shannon, and Jay thinks we can serve the divorce papers on Friday. That's all that's going on." Tali tries to smile a little.

Sydney reaches for Tali's hands and says, "Wow, that's quite the download. Sounds like you have all the pieces of this puzzle accounted for. By the way, how did the Zoom call with Gordon Silvers go this past Thursday?"

"It was fine. Typical Gordon. The design is coming along per our agreed-upon schedule. I'm meeting Mamita at the yacht club for lunch on Friday. He'll be there. I'll follow up and let you know."

"Sounds good," Sydney says. "What's on your schedule for today?"

"I completed the Convention Center augmentations. They are ready for your review. I'll have the other three project updates and timelines on your desk by late afternoon. Plus,

I scheduled a much-needed lunchtime workout with Ryan. I just need to get back on track..." Tali is interrupted by a knock on Sydney's door.

"Come in," says Sydney. Beth, her assistant, brings in a bouquet of flowers so large that only her arms and lower half of her chartreuse skirt can be seen.

"Oh my goodness, what's this for?" Sydney inquires.

Beth answers from behind the foliage, "These flowers were just delivered for Tali."

Tali stands and takes the massive bouquet. She places the vase on the conference table and searches for a card, which she reads aloud. "To my beautiful Tali. I love you always. I'll call tonight. Love, Blake"

Tali throws the card down on the table, saying, "Of all the nerve. He's a piece of work. This, ladies, is called 'Hoovering.' It's what narcissists do when they feel that their victim supply is evaporating...leaving them without a source for their ego boosts and rages and getting their jollies from cutting someone down constantly to make themselves feel more grand. He sent me my favorite flowers to try to 'hoover me'—just like the vacuum cleaner—to recover and contain me again. I didn't even know about this kind of thing until I started working with my therapist to try to understand what Blake's been doing to me. I'm sorry."

Beth and Sydney tell Tali that no apologies are needed, and they ask how they can be helpful.

"I feel so blessed to have you ladies in my life...to have a boss and work team so caring is rare. Okay. I better get to my office to finish those design updates I promised you, Sydney. Beth, could you come to my office to pick up the Convention Center augmentations and take them to Sydney? I'll grab this monstrosity of a bouquet. It will be a warm-up for my workout with Ryan in a few hours." Everyone chuckles. Beth follows Tali to her office to retrieve the file.

7

It's Time

Tali drives to her townhouse after work the following day, delighted to be greeted by Jasper with her usual vigor and Misty with her laid-back purr and brush against Tali's leg. Tali accepts the attention with gracious pats and hugs. She puts her briefcase in her studio and returns to the master suite to change clothes. She heads to the kitchen for a water bottle. It's around 7:00 p.m., a good time to walk Jasper on the beach.

As she passes Tia's Beach Café, she notices it's still open. Then she remembers that Tia stays open later on Wednesdays for a local church group to eat and mingle after their Wednesday evening Bible studies. Tali waves to Tia as she and Jasper pass by. Tia motions for Tali to come to the patio, which Tali is delighted to do. They hug, and Tia bends down to pat Jasper before introducing Tali to everyone on the patio. They invite Tali to sit down and dine with them.

"I wouldn't want to impose," Tali says.

"We insist."

Tia pulls over a chair for Tali and retrieves a water bowl and snacks for Jasper. They enjoy a delicious dinner and an inspiring conversation with the beautiful setting sun over the Pacific Ocean. Tali thinks *I needed this, God. Thank you.* As the evening concludes, Tali expresses her gratitude for the wonderful fare and new friends.

"Come back next Wednesday," says Tia, "We'll all be here."

"I just might," says Tali, then says, "I don't have my wallet since I was just taking Jasper for a walk."

"It's on the house." She hugs Tali tightly. "I love you, you know," Tia says.

"I love you too," says Tali. She and Jasper say goodbye and begin their walk back to the townhouse.

Tali's phone has been on silent the entire evening. She looks at it when she gets home and sees eight text messages and four voicemails from Blake. It's now 9:00 p.m. The instant she turns her phone on, it rings. It's Blake. Her attorney says not to talk with Blake until after he's served on Friday so as not to hint that anything legal is going on. She ignores the call. The voicemail notification tone sounds.

Blake texts her: "Where are you? Are you home? Are you okay? I'm worried about you. Call me."

She texts to get him off her back: "I'm fine. Long day. I'm tired. Good night."

He texts back: "Okay, babe. Good night. Love you. xoxo"

Tali gets the pets settled, brushes her teeth, and climbs into bed. She looks at her phone to set the alarm, then decides to listen to Blake's voicemails.

With each message, his voice becomes louder until he screams, "Where the hell are you, Tali? Why aren't you answering my calls? Who are you with? I'll call you again in a few minutes. You better answer."

Tali closes the voicemail app as tears stream down her cheeks. She emails Jay Richards with updates on Blake's assaults on her and sends audio copies of the voicemails. She requests a phone call with Jay in the morning.

Jay is working late and immediately emails her back: "How about 8:00 a.m. tomorrow?"

Tali replies, "Perfect. Thanks, Jay."

"Of course. I look forward to it."

Tali extinguishes the light. Jasper and Misty are snoozing on her bed. Tali's mind is churning with thoughts about Blake's raging messages, meeting Jay, her session tomorrow with Shannon, and Mamita's arrival. That last sweet thought allowed her to drift off to sleep.

8

Who Can You Call?

It's Thursday morning. Tali's alarm sounds at 6:00 a.m. She gets up, makes coffee, and takes Jasper for a quick walk. She settles the pets, prepares herself for work, and then calls Sydney. "I have a call with the divorce attorney at 8:00 a.m. I'll be in the office by 10:00."

"Fine. Let's meet as soon as you get in to review your files."

"Sounds good." At 8:00 a.m., Tali's in her upstairs studio with the financial documents that Bentley and his dad helped her put together and the investment details that the finance guy at work helped her with yesterday.

Jay calls, and they review the documents. Jay has a list of items he needs to finish putting together the divorce papers that afternoon if they want to serve the documents to Blake tomorrow in Monterey. Jay informs Tali about what's involved in Community Property Law in California. They finish the call with plans to follow up first thing tomorrow morning.

Tali enters her office at 9:45 a.m. and goes directly to Sydney. They catch up on how Tali's doing and Jay's call, and jump into the review of Tali's designs. Tali takes notes and answers Sydney's questions. They wrap up at 11:15 a.m. Tali meets with Beth for a few minutes to review Sydney's comments, and they schedule some follow-ups with clients. She and Beth confirmed they can get closure on Sydney's action items by the end of the day on Monday. When Tali returns to her office, she sees another bouquet...red roses this time...four dozen...from who else but Blake. Tali picks up the vase of flowers and takes it to the reception area. She removes the card and places the vase on a table in the lobby near some chairs with red and sage cushions. The flowers add a lovely organic accent to the space.

Well, she thinks, *I wouldn't want to waste four dozen red roses. When Blake hoovers, he doesn't spare any expense.*

9

Finding Faith in Safe Places

Tali arrived early for her weekly therapy appointment with Shannon. In a few minutes, the administrative assistant leads her down the hall to Shannon's office.

I'm grateful to have this safe place, Tali thinks as she sits in the well-worn leather recliner, creased in spots like an old baseball glove needing an application of saddle soap. She looks around and realizes she has almost memorized the framed diplomas and certificates of recognition professionally hung in a cluster. This morning, her attention focuses on a cross about eighteen inches tall by a foot wide. It is the only item hanging on the wall opposite the certificates. Two dozen words of encouragement were inscribed on the cross, including a few common Biblical-related sayings. She had been passively aware of it in previous counseling sessions as part of the office décor, but for some reason, today, the words seemed to leap off the cross into her heart: BELIEVE, FAITH, LOVE, TRUST, and REJOICE.

Her eyes scanned the groupings of words. The one that said GOD HEARS OUR PRAYERS caused Tali to say a quick prayer as she recognized the familiar click, click, click of Shannon's always-stylish shoes on the tile floor heading to the office. Her heart was heavy with all the emotional turmoil, and she felt a wave of empathy from the words on the cross.

As the door opened, Shannon greeted Tali with a professional but personal "Hi, there, Tali. How are we doing today?"

Tali murmured, "I'm here."

Shannon responds quietly, "Tell me what's happened."

Tali relays the recent scenes with Blake pinning her against the car at the restaurant in Newport Beach and the surrounding details. She added, "My memory of the night when I woke up bleeding on the bathroom floor came back when Blake had me pinned against the car. He lied to me about that night, saying I'd fallen. Now I remember him shoving me, causing me to hit my head on the towel rack and leaving me lying there unconscious. He's hurt me too much, Shannon."

Shannon goes radio silent for several minutes before saying measured words. "Tali, your situation with Blake has now escalated to a level where I need to speak to you not only as a counselor to a client but also as one woman to another. . Your safety, both physical and emotional, is a priority. You've mentioned your belief in God, His role in your life, and your supportive family and friends. You'll need all of that and more as you move forward. You are at a critical decision point in your marriage to Blake."

Tali responds quickly. "I contracted with a well-known divorce attorney named Jay Richards and put together the financial information he needs to serve papers to Blake."

"I'm familiar with Jay Richards, having had other clients who used him to separate their lives and move forward. I think you are in good hands. And I'm here for you, whatever decisions you make."

After Shannon and Tali discuss additional details of the past few weeks, Shannon suggests that Tali continue to develop a no-contact strategy with Blake to help her avoid Blake's control tactics.

She explains, "Narcissists tend to go into a panic mode as they lose power over a spouse or partner. They fear losing them because they are their source of power. Relationships are necessary to recharge their battery. It's especially important to call 911 if you ever feel that Blake is putting you in physical danger. Always keep your phone handy and have a couple of friends on standby. Finally, I hope you don't think it will all go smoothly or fast. Since you are dealing with a narcissist, the legalities of divorce get complicated, and it could take some time."

"I'll do my best to sustain a no-contact position, especially now that he's assaulted me again. He won't make it easy."

"No, he won't. Remember, you're smarter and stronger than you imagine, but he will do everything he can to keep you under control. Take care, and I'll see you next week."

* * * * *

At 2:00 p.m., Tali meets with the finance/investment expert at the interior design firm where she works. He helps her put investment details together for the Statement of Position and Statement of Income and Expenses document so she can complete the petitioner's filing for divorce tomorrow.

* * * * *

At 6:00 p.m., Tali drives home from work. Mamita is already there and has taken Jasper for an evening walk and fed and watered both pets. As Tali enters the garage, a delivery truck from Tali's favorite restaurant pulls up in front of her townhouse. The delivery person rings the front doorbell. Mamita answers the door as Tali walks into the townhouse. "Who's at the door?" she inquires.

Mamita replies, "Dinner is being delivered. Did you order something?"

"No. He must have the wrong address," Tali replies. Mamita and the delivery person walk into the dining room and show Tali the invoice for the order, which has already been paid in full. Tali looks at the invoice. It's over $300.

"This is from Blake. Of course, my favorite restaurant." She looks at the delivery man and smiles. "Thank you, but please deliver this beautiful meal to someone else...would your family like it?" she asks the delivery man."

"Yes, ma'am...but are you sure? This cost a lot of money."

"Please, take it. Please take it to your family."

"I'm not sure..." he hesitates.

I'll call the restaurant and tell them you are delivering the meal to another address and will be delayed returning to work this evening."

"Thanks. Actually, this is my last delivery for the day. After this, I drive the truck back to the restaurant and then go home to my family. Thank you so much!"

Tali says, "Enjoy the meal!"

The delivery man leaves. Mamita puts her arm around Tali's shoulder and says, "I'm so proud of you. That was such a nice thing to do."

Tali replies, "Thanks Mamita. Knowing it was another of Blake's control games to try and hoover me back, I couldn't enjoy that meal. Makes me sick just thinking about him and his antics."

Mamita says, "I'm here for you. What do you want to do for dinner?"

"You've been working and traveling today. Could we eat here tonight? I've got some fresh swordfish steaks in the fridge that I picked up yesterday, Caesar salad ingredients, and maybe some baked new potatoes. Does that sound good?"

"That sounds wonderful. How about you get comfortable, and I'll start getting everything together?"

Tali hugs Mamita. Tears are falling as she thanks her for being with her. "I need you. I love you."

"I love you too, my dear. I'm here as long as you need me to be."

Tali gets into comfy clothes and returns to the kitchen, where Mamita gathers the ingredients. Tali lights a candle, and the two ladies begin seasoning the fish and tossing the salad. Mamita preps and places the new potatoes in the oven. Tali opens a sauvignon blanc to share while cooking dinner and catching up on family news.

Mamita tells Tali, "Roman will be home from veterinary school in St. Kitt's for a break."

"Wonderful. How's my little brother doing?"

"He's doing well. He's considering specializing, but is unsure since he just began the program last fall. His work at a veterinary clinic in Mission Viejo during the summers while he was in college was useful."

"You know the two of us lost touch," Tali says quietly.

"Yes. I never knew why or what happened. You two were so close growing up, and then you went to college and got busy with the tennis team, and he got busy in high school with football and track. Guess you two just kind of drifted apart..." Mamita notices that Tali's crying again. "Oh dear, did I say something wrong?"

"No, Mamita," Tali speaks through the tears. "Blake was so jealous of how close I was to Roman. I could tell him anything, and he felt the same about me. Roman told me Blake yelled at him and told him to leave me alone. Blake threatened him. So, Roman decided to avoid the friction and leave me alone. I'm so angry Blake drove Roman out of my life. I miss my little brother so much. I would like to see him and talk with him. When is he coming home?"

"He'll be home for a week in two weeks. Let's get you two together and repair some of the brokenness Blake has caused." Mamita pauses, then adds, "I had no idea. I would have stepped in and given Blake a piece of my mind."

"No, Mamita. It's okay. That would only have made it worse. Then Blake would have driven you out of my life as well."

"Oh, baby girl, don't worry, *that* would never happen. *No one will ever drive me away from you!*"

Tali says, "I love you."

Mamita replies, "I love you too, my dear. I think the grill's ready. I'll put the fish on. Do you want to check the potatoes?"

Tali grabs a paper napkin to wipe her eyes as she opens the oven and turns over the potatoes. "They're almost done."

Tali and Mamita finish cooking and set the terrace table. They enjoy a nice dinner and talk about everything...except Blake...his name never comes up in their personal and professional artist–interior designer conversations. After dinner, they clean up and put away leftovers before settling on the terrace with coffee. Tomorrow, Mamita will be touring local art galleries, and they arrange to meet at the yacht club for lunch. Tali hopes she might introduce her mother to Gordon Silvers if he's on-site.

They say goodnight, and Mamita climbs the stairs to the guest room, where Misty and Jasper are already waiting for her. "These pets are such nice little hostesses," she acknowledges before settling in.

Tali gets into bed and checks her phone. Blake has been texting and calling to brag about the expensive dinner he ordered and delivered. Tali is about to put the phone on the charger in her bedroom when a text from Bentley appears.

"Want to chat?"

Tali calls him immediately. "Hi."

"How are you?"

"Doing okay. Miss you."

"Miss you too."

"Is Mamita there?"

"Yes. It's so lovely having her here with me. We cooked dinner here tonight.

"Nice."

"You'll never guess what Blake did!"

"What did he do this time? Is he there?"

"No. He's in Monterey."

"Ok, good. What did he do?"

"He ordered my favorite meal from my favorite restaurant and spared no expense on appetizers...multiple entrees...wine and desserts...to the tune of $300, and had it delivered to my townhouse!"

"No way!"

"Yes, way!"

"Was it good?"

"I sent it away with the delivery guy to share with his family. He was so appreciative."

"That was sweet."

"I just didn't want it to go to waste. He's also sent dozens of flowers to my office this week. Our lobby...reception area...break room...conference rooms...are all decorated with expensive floral accents right now...thanks to Blake and his 'hoovering' tactics. It's so sad that he's clueless."

"Well, he does have a personality disorder."

"That's what he's clueless about." They both laugh.

"Wanna talk this weekend? Tesca's out of town on business. Think I'll hang out with some buddies after work."

"Sounds good. I'll give you the scoop tomorrow after Blake's served with the divorce petition. Get ready...he may call you."

"Oh, okay. Thanks for the heads up. You stay strong. Call me if you need me."

"Thanks. I'll call you. I'm glad Mamita is here in case Blake shows up."

Bentley says, "I'll call my buddies at the North Beach police station to have a car in front of your place for a few days starting tomorrow...just in case. I want you and Mamita to be safe. Love you, Turt."

"Thanks, Bentley. Love you, too."

"Nite."

"Nite nite."

10

He's Served

Early Friday morning, Tali and Mamita take Jasper for a walk, stopping to talk to Tia at the café. Tali is nervous about the day ahead. She goes to work and then talks to Jay on the phone. The divorce petition is ready to go.

Tali and Mamita meet at the yacht club for lunch. Tali sees Gordon Silvers and waves to him.

"Good afternoon," Tali greets them. "This is my mother, Jackie.

Gordon says hello and introduces LeeAnn. "My wife is here," he says curtly, "because I left my credit card on the night-stand ordering new pocket squares last night. She should have noticed that before I left for work."

LeeAnn acknowledges both women, then turns back to Gordon. "Really? You're mad at me? I left a meeting with donors at the museum to run home and get your credit card because you said it was urgent. Why are *you* angry?"

Gordon replies, "I'm just having a bad day. That's all. I'll make it up to you. Wanna go out to dinner tonight? Just the two of us? Get a babysitter for the children?"

LeeAnn sighs, "Okay. I'll call Natalie. She's home from college this weekend, and the children would love to see her."

Gordon quickly kisses her and walks away, saying he needs to get to a meeting.

The three women stand there awkwardly. "I apologize," LeeAnn says. "He's being a bit difficult today. He gets this way. I try to keep the peace, if you know what I mean."

"Oh, I know what you mean," says Tali. "I heard you say something about a museum. Do you work at a local museum?"

"Yes. I am Assistant Curator at the Newport Beach Art Museum. I was meeting with donors when I got Gordon's urgent message about needing a credit card. He has others...sorry... I shouldn't be venting to you. I don't even know you."

"It's okay. I can relate." Tali offers. "Believe me. My mom and I would love to visit your art museum while she's in town. One day next week? We could go to lunch after the tour if that suits your schedule?"

"That would be lovely. We have some new installations I want to get on display for this weekend's exhibition. Let me know when you'd like to tour the museum. I look forward to it. I apologize for rushing off. I need to get back to work. Here's my card. Call me later, and we can set up a time to meet. Nice meeting you both. Have a great day!"

Tali and Mamita say goodbye and then head to the restaurant for lunch. They're seated at a table by the window overlooking the marina. As they peruse the menu, Mamita asks Tali about her new design ideas for this space. Tali shares her ideas, then adds, "I'm looking forward to seeing the new exhibits in the art museum. I haven't visited there since last year. It will be nice getting to know LeeAnn over lunch." She awaits Mamita's comments.

"Yes." She says very pensively, "Absolutely. She seems like a woman with a lot on her mind." They look at each other knowingly.

Just then, Gordon walks up to their table. "Hi again, I had to get to a quick meeting." He turns his attention to Mamita, reaching for her hand. "So you're Tali's mom."

"Yes," says Tali, "She's visiting from Mission Viejo for a few days. She's an artist. I think you'd like her work. I can bring samples from her portfolio to our next meeting."

Mamita says, "My daughter goes on. Mr. Silvers, your club is beautiful. I look forward to seeing the new designs you and Tali are working on."

Gordon says, "Very nice to meet you. And, yes, I've got some great new design ideas that Tali will implement. I'll influence her well, and working with me will increase her reputation. I've made quite a name for myself."

Mamita replies, "Congratulations."

"Enjoy your lunch, ladies. Tali, I'll see you here Monday to review the requested changes. Will you have those drawings ready for me to critique?"

"Yes, sir, Mr. Silvers. I'll see you here Monday."

He walks away. The ladies quietly look at each other, consciously saving their discussion about Mr. Silvers for later.

Hearing a notification on her phone, Tali tells Mamita that Jay just let her know Blake has been served with the divorce petition. She quickly emails back to express her thanks and affirm that she would like to talk with him this afternoon.

Within thirty seconds, Blake calls Tali's cell. Her phone's on silent, so it just buzzes. She ignores it for now. Then, the texts from Blake begin to appear. She ignores the messages, wanting to talk with Jay before she communicates with Blake. The two ladies finish their lunch, and Tali heads back to work. Mamita returns to the townhouse to hang out with the pets and take Jasper to the beach. She and Jasper stop by Tia's café for ice water and casual conversation. They arrive back at the townhouse around 4:30 p.m. Tali arrives home shortly after, and they decide to go out for dinner.

11

Surprise!

When Tali and Mamita return home from dinner, they find Blake sitting on the end of the leather couch with a beer, his laptop and an empty pizza box. Jasper chews on a pizza crust on the floor next to him. Misty is sitting on the hearth room windowsill.

"Hi! Thought I'd surprise you just like you surprised me today!"

"What do you mean?" Tali inquires.

"Oh, you know what I mean. What the hell, Tali? Why did you hire an attorney? And how did you come up with the numbers in the financials...you don't know shit about financial stuff. Who put you up to this? Was it you?" He glares at Mamita.

She begins to reply, but Tali brushes her arm and whispers to her. Then Tali says, "Blake, no one put me up to anything. I decided to file for divorce. It's my own decision."

"Ya, sure it is," he says. "You're not smart enough to pull this off. I will rip this up, and we'll forget this was ever done."

She says, "You have thirty days to respond, or you'll be in contempt."

"Oh...now you're using big bad legal words. Wow, Tali, you're something else. Okay then. I'm going to go to bed and sleep on this. You should do the same and we'll talk rationally in the morning. You'll see my point of view." He stands up, picks up his laptop, beer, and phone, and walks into the master suite, closing the double doors behind him.

"I know I should ask him to leave," Tali admits, "but I'm not ready for that confrontation. I'm tired. And Jay warned me I must be careful what I say and do around Blake."

Mamita nods, "Just as well. You do what you need to do."

Tali walks over to Jasper to pat her and then picks up Blake's trash...pizza box...messy napkins...and another empty beer bottle. She takes it to the kitchen, quietly disposing of it all.

Tali and the pets sleep in her art studio/office, and Mamita retires to the guest room. She texts Tali's dad good night and assures him that their daughter is strong. "I'm so glad I'm here, especially with Blake showing up unexpectedly." They text good night.

As Mamita extinguishes the light, she prays for a restful night to help her daughter weather Blake's "storm" tomorrow.

12

Do You Love Me?

(A question often asked by narcissists.)

Mamita walks into the kitchen with Jasper's leash at 8:00 a.m. She woke up early and took Jasper on a walk to the beach. Tali is walking down the stairs after sleeping in her art studio.

The master suite doors are open, and the bed is made. Blake's bags are still on the floor next to his side of the bed, but he's nowhere to be found. Suddenly, he walks through the garage entry door into the kitchen, whistling, and says, "Good morning, ladies! Hope your rest was peaceful." He's carrying a tray with three to-go cups of coffee and a bag bulging with something that smells savory. "I went for a run this morning and decided to pick up breakfast for us while I was out. Man, what a good run! I'm more fit than ever! Anyway, let's take all this out to the terrace. Mamita, could you grab some placemats and napkins? Tali, could you get some utensils out? I'll carry the coffee and food outside."

Tali and Mamita are puzzled by Blake, who acts as if Tali hadn't served him with divorce papers yesterday. They take the linens and utensils to the terrace for the brunch Blake has set out. After everyone is seated, Blake raises his coffee cup to toast to a beautiful morning, a beautiful wife, her Mamita, and a beautiful future together. Tali starts to speak, and Blake glares at her. He continues, "Honey, I know we can work everything out. You didn't have to bring an attorney into our marital life... basically, you're inviting the legal system into our bedroom."

Mamita looks up from her bagel at that moment and turns toward Tali.

"Blake, I'm done. You've attacked me more than once. The first time in the bathroom. You lied to me, leaving me bleeding on the floor. And at the restaurant parking lot. My attorney says the police were called after I drove away. I don't know how you talked your way out of that one. I do know you have thirty days to respond to the divorce petition."

Blake is silent for a long time, then says, "Tali, you're making a big mistake battling me on this. We should go to counseling. We can work this out. I know we can."

"I've tried to get you to go to counseling with me in the past. You've always said that our relationship issues are my fault and that I'm too emotional and overly sensitive. Let's end this."

She gets up, takes Mamita by the hand, and the two ladies leave the terrace, using Jasper as an excuse for another walk.

Blake sits there alone for a while, finishing his bagel and coffee. He's upset and wonders again if any of this could be his fault, but the voice in his head redirects his thoughts. *Don't get all pathetic. You can manage this the way you do everything else.*

You always have options! He sighs, then walks inside to grab his laptop and phone. He calls an old college buddy who's been divorced twice since college. Blake figures he will know a thing or two. They talk for an hour, and Cody shares a few names. Blake thanked him and began searching online for divorce attorneys in Monterey. He emails two possible firms to schedule a phone call on Monday.

Then, he calls his brother, Thomas, to complain about Tali. "Thomas, you must keep the divorce filing a secret until I can talk Tali out of it."

"What if you can't?"

"I have a few ideas on how to scare her into dropping the case."

"You know I can help with both ideas and if you need to take action. The security field I'm in has access to many resources."

"Good to know. If nothing else, we can make Tali afraid of being alone and running out of money. I'll use her ignorance of financial matters to my advantage. Blake says, "I'm just waiting for Tali to crash and burn. Which she will when I make her call off this silly divorce."

The brothers both laugh. He and Thomas devise a scheme. Thomas is unexpectedly excited about bringing Tali down.

About that time, Tali, Mamita, and Jasper walk back into the townhouse.

"How was your walk, ladies?" Blake asks.

"It was very nice," says Mamita. Tali is silent as she walks onto the terrace to find everything left on the table. Insects have found the brunch leftovers. She gathers the food and coffee cups to dispose of and puts the table linens in the washer.

* * * * *

Tali talked with Jay while she and Mamita were walking. He advised her to say as little to Blake as possible since Blake said he would fight her during the divorce process. "Don't give him anything to use against you. If he tries to start a conversation about financial matters, don't engage."

Blake walks into the laundry room and says, "Tali, let's go to dinner tonight and discuss this matter alone. I need to talk with you privately. We can work this out."

"Mamita is only visiting for a few more days. I won't be rude and leave her here alone while you try to wine and dine me. I'm not playing your game. I need you to leave."

He says, "I plan to drive back to Monterey tomorrow afternoon. I really should stay longer to talk with you, but I can't. They can't function without me, so I must get back. My boss has it out for me. He's jealous of me. I just don't get it. I think circles around him and everyone there."

She looks at him in disbelief. "I'd prefer it if you would drive back to Monterey this afternoon. I have nothing to say, and Mamita and I have plans."

Blake stares at her, his eyes growing dark.

"I mean it, Blake. Please leave."

He grabs his bags and huffs out of the townhouse. While driving, he calls Thomas, Molly, and Bentley, but no one answers. Left to his thoughts, he rationalizes everything. *Place yourself firmly in control,* the voice says. *Plot ways to terrify Tali. You know how weak she is. She's mental. She'll fall apart, but only if you manage her. Go back to Monterey and leave her and her mommy to themselves. They deserve each other.*

* * * * *

On Monday, he's back at work, busy making phone calls to attorneys. The first one, Pamela, seems to be a good fit. He tells her about the claims Tali is making about him.

"I'm none of those things." He tells Pamela, "Someone else is making Tali believe the lies about me and advising her to get a divorce. Her mental state is, at best, unstable." He uses the same pitch during his interview with two more attorneys in the afternoon, still thinking Pamela could be the right fit as his attorney to fight Tali in the divorce process.

13

Dinner and Diatribes

Blake hires Pamela as his attorney on Tuesday and invites her for dinner. They arrive at the restaurant at approximately the same time and introduce themselves. Pamela wears a tailored teal pantsuit tastefully accessorized with silver bangles and earrings. Her wavy auburn hair is coiffed at shoulder length, beautifully framing her chiseled features.

Blake immediately notices her intoxicating smile as she reaches to shake his hand. They walk with the hostess to Blake's requested out-of-the-way table, where they can speak freely without other patrons overhearing their confidential conversation. Pamela listens and takes notes on her iPad as they await drinks and appetizers. Blake talks about his marriage, how he's always taken care of everything, and that Tali deserves nothing.

Pamela has dealt with clients like Blake previously. She immediately identifies him as a malignant narcissist and makes notes to that effect, careful that Blake cannot view her iPad screen. She'll let her boss at the law firm know that this client will be a headache to represent. She knows she's up for the challenge, having recently divorced her ex, who's also a malignant narcissist. She wonders what Tali is really like, but she will have to wait until the first group meeting of clients and attorneys to converse with Tali, and that will only be within a formal settlement/deposition setting. Pamela has a feeling, though, that Tali is not in the least the ignoramus that Blake portrays her to be. Pamela duly listens to Blake and his proposed strategies, which he believes are on-point since speaking with his college buddy about his two divorces.

"I'm pretty smart, Pamela, and it wouldn't take much for me to become an expert on California divorce law. I probably don't need an attorney, but it looks good to have a representative if this thing goes to court. Right?"

"Right," says Pamela, finishing her notes and closing her iPad. She is glad the evening is over.

That night, Blake builds a Statement of Position and Statement of Income and Expenses for his and Tali's assets, liabilities, annual income streams, and annual expenses. He told Pamela that he'd have those documents ready by Thursday morning. He texted Tali to say that he'd hired an attorney and to reply to his message if she was still seriously considering trying to divorce him.

Tali responds immediately, "Yes, I'm divorcing you."

He replies. , "Okay. Let's schedule a FaceTime call tomorrow evening after I finish my work. I know you're more flexible with your schedule. All you do is draw pictures for people. It's a nice hobby, Tali. I'll be finished with my important clients at 6:00 p.m. tomorrow. We can talk then. Make sure you're available. xoxo"

Tali replies. , "My job is not a hobby."

Blake texts, "You're so cute. Of course it is."

Tali texts, "I cannot talk with you without my attorney present."

Blake replies, "Sure you can. He'll never know."

Tali replies, "Call your attorney and schedule a conference call with all of us. Goodbye, Blake."

Blake calls her cell. Tali does not pick up the call.

He texts her: "Pick up my call!"

She stares at her buzzing cell phone. Five minutes later, he texts: "I'll talk with my attorney, Pamela, about setting up a video conference call with you, me, her, and your attorney. I look forward to seeing you. I miss your beautiful smile. I wish I could hold you and kiss you right now. xoxo"

Tali emails Jay about Blake's text messages to her. Jay asks her to screenshot the texting conversation and send the pictures to him, which she does.

He's building a file on Blake's chaotic and erratic behaviors. Jay asks himself if this guy is for real and knows he must help Tali come out from under Blake's narcissistic abuse and control. They'll need a bulletproof case.

Dear Josie, Thank goodness I have Jay to help me. And I have my tribe...Mamita, Daddy, Molly, Bentley, Ben, Candace, Sydney, Ryan, and Tia. I know Roman and I can repair our brother-sister relationship that Blake tried to destroy. I'm praying to God that we'll all come through this experience for the better and not for the worse.

* * * * *

Jay emailed Tali with some financial questions the following day, cc'ing his assistant, Mallory. Tali texted Bentley for advice on how to respond to Jay's questions. They agreed to talk on FaceTime later that afternoon.

On Thursday morning, Mamita drives back home to Mission Viejo.

14

Expert Advice

Doubts and questions begin to consume Tali. She's grateful to be meeting with Shannon, who shares valuable information about post-narcissistic abuse stress disorder, and defines symptoms and triggers.

"The narcissist's primary goal is to take a strong person and break them down. It's as if they suck the spirit out of them. This aftermath/stress disorder can occur when you leave a narcissistic, abusive relationship. You need to be aware of these symptoms when they arise: feeling doubtful, confused, unable to trust yourself or others, and getting panic flashbacks. Your instinctive defense is to shut down emotionally to avoid feeling pain and to disconnect from your feelings, which the narcissist has too often ridiculed. How frequently did Blake describe you as being too emotional and overly sensitive?"

"All the time," Tali acknowledges.

"There are many physical symptoms, the same that are caused by any chronic stress. It isn't easy to make decisions. You have low self-esteem, which causes you to withdraw from people. You fear being judged. As abuse continues, mood extremes can form without any apparent cause. Does this resonate with you?"

"All of it. And I have nightmares."

"It's important to understand the idea that narcissists tend to have a voice in their head. Narcissists are pathological, empty beings who can change their colors from one moment to the next without any indication as to why."

"Welcome to my world."

"No longer!" Shannon asserts. "You are taking charge of your life, leaving Blake and rebuilding your self-esteem."

"It will take a village. I do have an amazing group of supporters who love me. I call them my tribe."

"Excellent. I hope I am included in that tribe."

"Definitely."

15

You're the Worst...
wait for it... wait for it...
Want Some Coffee?

lake drives to Newport Beach unannounced on Friday after work. Tali had not changed the locks, fearful that might
make him aggressively angry. That night he showed up,
hoovering her with compliments, asking about her work, and
being his most charming.

She couldn't keep him from coming, but she could remove
herself. Tali is afraid of being alone with Blake, so when he goes
out on the terrace, she texts Molly to ask if she and the pets can
stay with her and Chad tonight.

Molly immediately replies, "Yes, of course. Are you okay?"

Tali texts, "Thanks. Yes. I'll explain when I get there. Like in
forty-five minutes?"

Molly says, "Sure thing. I'll have the back garage open for you. Come on in."

Tali texts, "Thanks. See you soon."

Tali gets her overnight bag. When Blake enters the garage, she is packing her car and gathering the pets.

"Hey, what are you doing? I'm here this weekend so that we can talk and work out this whole frivolous divorce thing you're instigating. Tali, you're delusional. I'm concerned about you, and I want to help you. Honey, let's go back inside where we can talk."

She says, "No. I'm leaving right now. Call your attorney and have her talk to my attorney. Blake, I'm done. You're not going to hurt me anymore."

He stands there, puzzled, as his eyes darken and his face reddens. Before he can start screaming at her, she and the pets leave. He stands there for a few moments, unable to process the situation quickly, then walks back into the townhouse, grabs a beer out of the fridge, a koozie out of the pantry, and then goes to his favorite spot on the leather couch. It has indentations from him always sitting in the same spot. He turns on his laptop and grabs the remote to turn on the TV.

He texts Molly. No response. He texts Bentley. No response. He calls his mom. After twenty minutes of listening to her talk about herself, and not asking him how he's doing, he regrets dialing her number. He finally gets a word in and tells her he will call her back tomorrow. He sits there staring at the TV. A moment of hopelessness hits him, but the voice in his head is at the ready. *You're fine. You don't need that bitch. Or the damn pets. Just relax. Leave a voicemail for Tali, reminding her of all the times she's broken down. Rebuke her for not being perky and enthusiastic about his visit. Has she stopped loving me? Haven't you noticed she's not mentally stable? She'll never be able to manage the townhouse alone. Send her a text telling her to drop the divorce petition and move to Monterey.*

Blake texts but Tali does not reply. She screenshots Blake's text messages and emails the pics to Jay.

16

Call 911

After Tali arrives at Molly and Chad's house on Friday evening, Chad gets the pets settled and takes Tali's bag to the guest room. Molly and Tali hang out on the back patio. Molly listens as Tali talks about Blake's unexpected arrival. His hoovering. His rages. More hoovering. His "concerns" about her mental state.

Molly exclaims, "Tali, you're the most sane person I know! OMG. Blake's the one with the loose screw. He makes no sense."

Tali replies, "As far as narcissist playbooks go, Blake is a textbook. He's predictable, which is kind of scary. However, I didn't expect him to show up for the weekend after I asked him to leave last time. He's trying to make me drop the divorce petition and move to Monterey. He has an evil plan of completely isolating and controlling me, a lot like he did when I was recovering from the accident. Like he did with Roman. I can feel it." She takes a deep breath, adding, "Thanks for letting me and the pets stay here tonight. I need to stay away from Blake. I need to develop my strategy for addressing this situation head-on to protect myself."

Molly says, "You're so welcome. We love you and the pets. Stay as long as you need. Chad loves your cooking, by the way. If you want to stay tomorrow night and cook dinner for—I mean with—us, that's great." Molly smiles.

Tali says, "Yes, of course. Let's talk about menu ideas in the morning, and then we can go to the market. I'd absolutely love to cook with you tomorrow. It's good to have something simple to look forward to."

Molly says, "We love you and Jasper and Misty, and we'll do whatever we can to ease you away from your monster of a husband." Molly hugs Tali as they say their goodnights and go inside to both get some sleep.

Tali enters the guest room, where Jasper and Misty are already asleep. About an hour later, Tali awakens in a sweat after a nightmare about her recovery from her head-on collision with a wrong-way driver. She remembers a particular night during the healing process after the wreck, while she was still in a wheelchair before she learned to walk again. In her dream memory, she was talking with someone on the phone. Since she was still non-weight-bearing due to her broken legs, hips, and pelvis, she was trying to transfer from the wheelchair to the sofa on the sliding board, and she fell off the board onto the floor. She didn't feel like she reinjured anything. The day caretaker nurse had already left because Blake would arrive home soon. She stayed on the phone to have human contact with someone in case she had further injured herself, thinking that Blake would help her up when he got home.

In the dream, when he arrived and walked into the family room, he began screaming at Tali. "What happened? Why are you on the floor? Who are you talking to?" He was going into full-on rage.

She started crying and disconnected the call, asking Blake to help her back into her wheelchair. He refuses and goes into the master suite, slamming the doors behind him.

Then Tali recognizes the nightmare was something that really occurred. She remembers calling 911 to get help. The police arrived to find Blake there, doing nothing to help his injured wife get back into her wheelchair. The police helped Tali and asked her if she wanted to file a report claiming spousal neglect. She says not tonight and thanks the officers for their help. The vivid memory of Blake raging at her as she sat helpless in her wheelchair after the police left was excruciating. She wondered how many other things she'd forgotten.

The next morning, she tells Molly about the dream. "It actually happened that way." Tali admits for the first time.

Molly is mortified to hear about Blake's behavior while Tali fought to recover from the wreck. Tali realized she'd just told one of many secrets she'd kept to herself.

After going to the market and before starting to prepare dinner for Molly and Chad, Tali walks to the beach. She sits on a rock to think and write.

Dear Josie, We all make choices. I remember things I've blocked out, kept to myself, pretending everything was all right. I can't lie to myself about how Blake treats me anymore, and I can't keep his manipulation and controlling behaviors a secret.

17

Pontification and Deflection

The first settlement meeting is finally scheduled via Zoom. Jay and Tali are in a conference room in Newport Beach, while Blake and his attorney are in a conference room in Monterey.

Jay calls the meeting to order, only to be immediately interrupted by Blake pontificating while eating cheese and apple slices. He drones on about investments, pointing at Jay with his apple slice. Blake tells Jay, "You're just an old man with a grizzly voice. I can't imagine why you would take Tali's case except to take her money. She hasn't got a leg to stand on."

Pamela tries to return his attention to Jay's question, but Blake keeps talking about himself and blaming everyone else for anything that has happened. She's on alert, sensing that Blake's temper is rising.

Blake says, "Who's at fault for the supposed ruin of this relationship? That would be Tali, of course. She's an airhead, just like my mom always said. She's too emotional and too sensitive."

Jay interjects, "Blake, you have physically attacked Tali on multiple occasions. That is why she's petitioned you for a divorce. Let's focus on the financials, starting with the Newport Beach townhouse. We'll get it appraised; then you and Tali can decide who will buy whom out if you both agree to sell it on the market."

Tali writes a note on a legal pad and passes it to Jay. Jay says aloud, "Tali wants the townhouse. You live and work in Monterey and basically moved out when you took the new job. Both properties will need appraisals."

Blake whispers to Pamela.

Pamela says, "My client needs time to process this information. We'll schedule another Zoom meeting for next week." All agree and log off.

"Wow," says Tali. "Blake is going to try to take the townhouse from me, isn't he?"

Jay says, "Maybe. We'll be ready for whatever he and Pamela return with next week. In the meantime, let's talk about the assets you have listed on your Statement of Position. And, confidentially, of course, how's your job going? Any clues about the future for Tali Solace, interior designer?"

Tali says, "Sydney says I have partner potential. I'm young and still new in this profession. That said, I could be designing a space in Paris next year if the client likes the work I'm doing for her company here in the U.S. We'll see. I've been a little distracted with the divorce filing and Blake showing up unannounced these past two weekends. I have to focus and catch up on work this week. Is there anything I need to do on the divorce right now?"

Jay replies, "Not at this point. It's like a chess game. We wait for Blake's next move. You're going to be fine, Tali. Blake's a narcissistic ass, and what goes around comes around. Keep an eye on any charges on your joint credit card and bank account until we lock them. And be ready, he'll try to sabotage and smear you."

"Oh, he's already been trying to do that. Thankfully, I have a boss, friends, and family to help me shut down his antics and nonsense. I've learned a lot about how it feels to be gaslit, how to 'gray rock' when 'flying monkeys' swoop in so nothing interesting or remarkable is 'revealed' and how to divert a 'hoovering' situation. I never expected I'd need to learn how to deal with a psychopath—but here I am, married to one. How did this happen?"

Jay says, "Narcissists are experts at wearing a mask of deception to trick their victims into serious relationships. You're not alone, Tali. You're an intelligent empath. Narcissists prey upon intelligent empaths. We'll get you through this. Don't worry."

"Thanks, Jay," she says, trying to hide her fear. "I hope so."

"Stop by Mallory's office on your way out. She has some documents for you to sign."

Tali and Mallory talk while she signs the papers. Mallory says, "Jay is the best in these types of cases. You're in good hands." Tali hugs Mallory, thanks her for the encouraging words, and then leaves with more questions than answers.

18

Dear Josie...

After work, Tali goes home to hang out with Jasper and Misty. Bentley calls. They talk for a while. He's concerned about her. Later, she sits on the terrace with her journal.

Dear Josie...I'm so scared right now. Blake wouldn't finish the settlement meeting today when questioned about the townhouse. He's essentially already moved out! I'm afraid he will try to take my home away from me. He probably wants me to live under a bridge somewhere. Jay says Blake told Pamela he would take everything he could from me. I know it's community property law here, but Blake's so mean that he'll do anything to hurt me. I'm trying to compartmentalize this situation to get my mind back on my work. I have three design updates due next week. One of those is for yet another controlling person. Anyway, I digress. Jay says I must pay attention to Blake's expenditures in our joint accounts. I'm starting to see some patterns—almost like Blake's behaviors are becoming predictable. I've seen Blake behave in these ways when he felt underappreciated on his job. I'm beginning to figure out his playbook. It's more like a pamphlet since he repeats himself all the time. I'm having a hard time facing the dark reality of being in a relationship with a narcissist and potentially fighting the narcissist in court.

19

Blake Rages at His Attorney

Blake is sitting at his desk, staring out the window. He's so angry he can't focus on his work, but he hasn't been focusing on his work for a while now. He says aloud, "Damn you, Tali!" When the phone rings, he uses his nice voice.

"Hey Blake, it's Pamela."

Blake replies, "What's up?" Any news from the enemy?"

She notes his foul mood, replying, "No. Nothing from Jay. Have you decided if you want to fight her for the townhouse?"

He says, "Yes, of course I am. It's half mine. That bitch deserves nothing, I'm fighting her on everything. She has no right to try to divorce me. I'm the best thing that ever happened to her." His temper is rising.

Pamela starts talking calmly, "Now, Blake, you realize California is a community property state. She will get her due portion of the marital assets."

"I know," he screams. Then he turns toward the doorway to see coworkers staring at him. His boss is among them. Blake turns back toward the window and chastises Pamela, "You're no good, Pamela. How can you stick up for Tali? You're going to make me lose this divorce!"

She says, "Blake, calm down, I'm representing you. You know I'm a very successful attorney. You did your homework before you contacted me. I could tell by the questions you asked the first night we met. You'll be fine."

He says, "Fine is not good enough. I have to win! And make Tali regret ever filing for divorce." His eyes are black, and his face is red. "I have to go. I have a meeting in five minutes," he says, "But I have ideas for getting the townhouse away from Tali. Being in the financial industry, I have contacts with asset appraisers, including real estate appraisers. I'll talk to them and, if I have to, I'll bribe one of them to undervalue the townhouse property so that when I agree to buy out Tali, I won't have to pay much. And, she'll be befuddled as to why the property has diminished value. Plus, I've been talking with some of my overseas banking colleagues, and I have ways of moving some financial assets to overseas accounts where they will not be part of the divorce settlement. I know you'll keep my confidence, Pamela, because I pay you, and our fiduciary agreement states that sharing this type of information is attorney-client privilege. Gotta go." Blake ends the call.

Pamela sits at her desk, holding the phone in utter disbelief. "Oh, this is not good. Not good at all," she says to herself quietly.

20

Mr. and Mrs. Silvers

On Wednesday morning, Tali meets Gordon at the yacht club and then meets LeeAnn for lunch at the art museum tea room. The two ladies share a friendly hug when Tali walks into the tea room.

LeeAnn says, "Hi Tali! I'm so glad you could meet me for lunch today. Gordon told me this morning that he was scheduled to meet with you at the club today. How did that go?"

Tali replies, "It went okay. Gordon is requesting a few more modifications to the design plan. I think we're almost done with the design phase. Next comes ordering the décor selections and implementing the designs. It's always fun to see the plan come together!"

The two ladies smile and laugh—each knowing that Gordon can be difficult, but neither saying it out loud. The hostess leads them to a table by a window overlooking a small-scale version of the Gardens of Versailles.

"Wow!" Tali exclaims. "Those gardens are breathtaking!"

"Yes," LeeAnn agrees. "The museum's landscaper is quite phenomenal. He studied landscape architecture in Paris."

After listening to the server tell them about the specials, they peruse the menu. Each lady decides on one of the salads and iced water with lemon. Their conversation is light, to begin with. Tali asks about LeeAnn's children and new art exhibits. LeeAnn asks about design projects that Tali is working on and which artists pique her interest. Tali tells her Monet and Cezanne are her inspirations. She tells LeeAnn about her Mamita's talents with a paintbrush and her commercial artistry.

LeeAnn is intrigued and listens intently. "I met her briefly at the yacht club, didn't I?"

"Yes. We were sorry she didn't get to come here before she had to go home. Another time."

As the server delivers the meal, LeeAnn says grace and then casually asks Tali if she is married. Tali picks at her salad for a few seconds and then responds, "I'm currently divorcing my husband. He's exhibiting the traits of narcissistic personality disorder. He's attacked me multiple times. It's not a good relationship. I have a counselor and an attorney. It's amazing," she continues, "now that I've got a therapist and an attorney who are both well aware of and informed about NPD behaviors, I've learned just how thoroughly Blake exhibits them."

"Like what?" asks LeeAnn.

"Have you heard of 'love bombing,' 'gaslighting,' 'raging,' 'deploying flying monkeys,' and 'hoovering,' just to name a few?" She stops when she sees the expression on LeeAnn's face. Her mouth is open, and her eyes are a bit teary. "Oh no, LeeAnn," I'm so sorry. I've said too much. I'll be quiet."

LeeAnn says, "No, it's okay. It's just that I can relate. Gordon treats me and the children so harshly. He's always blaming us for his mistakes, and we're afraid of him. I'm sorry, Tali. I hardly know you, and my husband is your design client. I shouldn't be talking negatively about him. That's very unprofessional of me. Please forgive me." Tears are now leaking from the corners of her eyes.

Tali reaches across the table to touch LeeAnn's arm as she says, "I heard Gordon chastising you before at the yacht club. It caught my attention because it reminded me of Blake screaming at me, which he did daily. I felt sorry for you and hoped we would get the opportunity to chat one day. Now, here we are. There are no coincidences, LeeAnn. We were destined to cross paths. We can thank my boss, Sydney, for putting me on the design job at the club!"

LeeAnn smiles through the tears as she says, "Thanks Tali. I'm just not sure what to do. Gordon is a powerful man. The children and I are afraid of him. I can't leave him. Where would we go?"

Tali says, "Perhaps I can help. It's all so new to me. But I can see that you are a strong woman. Is Gordon a dangerous man? Does he beat you?"

"Sometimes," LeeAnn says. "He spanks the children at least once a week. They're good children. They don't deserve to be hit by him or anyone. I try to love on them as much as I can to try to buffer their dad's rampages and beatings." LeeAnn gets very quiet as she reviews all the times Gordon has made life so difficult for her and the kids.

21

Daddy's Home, Hide!

t is 6:12 p.m. when Gordon Silvers arrives at his mansion after a business trip. As predictable as clockwork, the cranking sound of the automatic garage door gets louder as the springs tense. The SUV coasts inside, and its driver-side door slams. The garage door retreats to its closed position, ending with a heavy thunk.

These are the sounds that LeeAnn fears the most. A foreboding feeling fills her, and she notices immediately that nine-year-old Ashley and her seven-year-old brother Andrew are already in motion. Instinctively, they run out of the kitchen into their bedrooms, grabbing some strewn toys in the family room, leaving Mom as their first line of defense.

Familiar footsteps announce his entrance through the back door. The dog and the cat quietly position themselves at their respective food bowls. Daddy pauses to pat the two heads that look up at him respectfully. He fills their bowls with economical food from the local chain big box warehouse.

He then glances around the open floor plan as an inspector would initially look over a possible crime scene to see if anything looks out of order.

The tone of his greeting to his wife of twelve years is dictated by whether or not there are dishes in the sink, a dishwasher not unloaded, toys not picked up, or anything else he may selectively call out to criticize. It is always his choice which card to play on any given day.

The next order of business is to see if dinner is being put on the table. Just as his own mother had done for his dad.

He utters a brief, gruff, unintelligible acknowledgment of his wife's existence, complete with no eye contact. He walks straight to the master bedroom, closing the door. His routine is to change from casual business clothes—a polo shirt and khakis—to homebody attire consisting of a tee shirt and athletic shorts.

Over the past several years, LeeAnn has schooled the children to listen for the master bedroom door closing and then to scurry silently to their assigned places at the table with hands prewashed.

When he returns, he takes his place at the head of the table and expectantly waits for each component of the meal to be plated and then passed to him. Tonight's fare is oven-grilled pork chops with rice and beans, no bread, no dessert. LeeAnn helps the children with their plates, and then she does her own.

She sits quietly, suppressing yet another round of routine anxiety. Her heart is racing, and she is almost nauseated as she waits for him to speak.

"So, dear, did you get everything done that we discussed earlier this morning?"

LeeAnn replies, "I put in a load of towels before I dropped off the children at school and went to work. Then I picked up the children at school, getting Ashley to her orthodontist appointment and Andrew to his fall baseball practice. I went by the store to get what we needed for dinner. I helped with homework while I cooked."

Dad picks up on the homework comment and asks, "Ashley, did you get any grades back on any papers today?"

"Yes, sir, Daddy," she says, mumbling.

"What were they?" he quizzed.

"An A minus in spelling...and a...and a...and a, uh...C on my math test."

Gordon raises his bushy eyebrows and shouts at her, "Ashley, how many times have I told you that not only is an A minus unacceptable, but now a C! That is just not tolerated in this family. You are a disgrace. Obviously, your mother is not helping either! I will be tutoring you at night on all your homework going forward! Do you understand me?"

LeeAnn interrupts, "Dear, how was work today?" LeeAnn had learned that if she could change the focus of the meal conversations from the children to her husband, it might spare a rage scene. His fits of rage are not relative to the severity of the mishap; they are all at the highest decibel level, red-faced, with blue eyes turning black. They are all laced with profanity and accusations, and take no prisoners.

The question about how his day went immediately turns the table into a monologue he scripted on the fly about how he is the smartest, most qualified, but most unrecognized and under-compensated person in the company. LeeAnn leans forward and quietly listens to every syllable as if she had never heard this diatribe from him before, even though she has heard it hundreds of times. He interrupts himself once to take the children to their rooms to do their homework. They both waste no time. Ashley camps out at the desk in her room while Andrew hides under his lower bunk bed.

Later, while LeeAnn clears the table, Gordon softly tiptoes to his daughter's room, walks in, and locks the door. He immediately starts where he left off at dinner, raging at her for ten minutes about how incompetent she is as a human being. And that she is grounded until her report card is all As.

He leaves her bedroom and heads toward the kitchen, where LeeAnn wraps up post-dinner kitchen cleanup.

He tells her, "Join me in the family room to watch a movie tonight."

Meanwhile, LeeAnn hears her daughter's muffled sobs from underneath her bedroom door down the hall. In her heart, she wants to stand in the gap for her daughter to shield her from her husband's wrath, but she knows from multiple previous efforts that it would only exacerbate the situation.

22

Communication

Blake emails Pamela to complain that Tali won't answer his calls and that she's not cooperating or communicating. Pamela calls him.

"That's how this works," Pamela tells him. "You and Tali are supposed to communicate through me and Jay."

"Well, that's not getting me what I need."

"Didn't Tali offer to let you stay in a motel nearby so you could have the pets for a visit?"

"Oh yeah, she texted me, 'Hey, let's schedule time for you to visit Jasper and Misty.' I texted back, saying, 'Don't call me Hey. My name is Blake.' It really aggravated me."

"You need to understand that all digital communications become part of the overall documentation."

"Now you tell me. You are the worst attorney!" Blake hangs up. His emotional state was waning, and he briefly considers giving up, giving in. The voice in his head erupts! *You don't give up. You don't give in. Pull yourself together.* After an hour passes with Blake deep in thought, he texts Tali to meet him halfway to talk.

Tali was willing to let him come to Newport Beach and stay in a hotel to visit the pets. Since he now wants her to drive and only wants to talk about the divorce, she offers to do a Zoom meeting next week with Jay and Pamela present.

She's still honing the art of communication with a narcis- · sist. Shannon and Jay have been coaching her on how to "gray rock," communicating with basically no emotion and no useful information. Tali can see how Blake uses this style, but it is so foreign to her. She's always been direct and clear in her communication. She's finding some levity in this matter since Blake is working to blindside, trick, and hoover her at every point. As Jay says, with a narcissist, these tactics will only intensify as the divorce process continues. He has encouraged Tali to take notes about Blake's behaviors. She recalls him saying that narcissists wear a mask and only have a limited number of plays in their playbook. The mask will begin to slip and Blake's feathers will become ruffled as Tali continues to walk away and no longer supply Blake's narcissistic needs as an ego-booster, admirer, rage victim, blame scapegoat, and sexual prey. She's done with those roles; however, she's still puzzled as to how all this happened. She knows Blake's childhood with a dominating mom was traumatic and she's always wanted to help him become stronger and more confident, but this endeavor has brought damage upon herself. Now she's trying to walk away from a relationship that she once thought was loving when it wasn't, while working to heal herself. She writes in her journal.

> *Dear Josie...This narcissistic personality disorder stuff is intense. I hope I can make it through this divorce without losing everything. I know Blake wants me to crawl back to him. I'm afraid of him. Shannon's been telling me to lean on my tribe, that people love me and want the best for me. I have to believe that. It's hard. I wake up every morning with fear and a knot in the pit of my stomach while I wonder what Blake's going to do to me today. Jay's telling me that we've got this case and that Blake's rages at his attorney, Pamela, are not helping his case. Pamela's so ready to finish this matter. Looks like we're going to court. That scares me. Oh, Josie. What's Blake gonna do next?*

23

More Insights

I n her weekly session with Shannon, Tali asks her to tell her more about NPD and how she can defend herself.

Shannon explains, "Narcissists are hypervigilant and despise apologies. Saying you're sorry is admitting a weakness. Any weakness is seen as an opportunity to break down any boundaries. They want you to believe that you're to blame for everything.

Psychologist and psychotherapist Carl Jung researched and introduced theories about the inner voice. Jung's work on universal mythic characters that reside within the collective subconscious of people the world over...evoking deep emotions... Ego, Soul, Self. There's an almost discernable pattern in the chaos of a narcissist. They expect submissive behavior at the same time that they despise it. They do create a lose-lose scenario for their victims."

"What should I do?"

"Right now, avoiding contact is the best tactic, and limiting communication to issues related to the divorce. He will never believe you really want to leave him. Why would anyone leave such a good-looking, confident, successful man?"

"I get it," says Tali, "or at least, I'm starting to."

"You are. And you're finding your inner strength. You've always been a nice person, haven't you, Tali?"

"I like people. I like to be nice, friendly, helpful, kind."

"Every one of those words you used to describe yourself is a negative for ego-driven people. They are flags that alert them that a victim is in the area, and their basic impulse is to take over, control, and manipulate. They do it with great charm and can ooze sweetness. That's the mythic mask. It's been around forever."

"Thank you. I think I'll do a little research myself and get more acquainted with this person I thought I would love and be with forever."

"You can do this, Tali!"

24

Siblings

Tali drives back to work after her session with Shannon. Her thoughts turn to her little brother, Roman. He's twenty years old (five years younger than Tali) and in his first year of vet school in St. Kitts, West Indies, which the American Veterinary Medical Association accredits.

When she and Mamita discussed their sibling relationship, Tali finally realized it began to disintegrate when she started dating and got serious about Blake. Mamita called Roman to tell him about Tali filing for divorce from Blake.

Tali's sitting on the chaise in her office, just thinking about all of this, when the phone buzzes. It's Roman. She answers, "Hey little brother. How's island life?"

Roman laughs a little and says, "I hear the weather's nice here, but I've been under a rock studying my eyes out with this vet school stuff!"

Tali smiles as she says, "Mamita says you're knocking it out of the park! I'm so proud of you!"

"Thanks, Sis," he says. "I hear you have some news going on there as well. Wanna talk about it? I'm sorry I've been incognito for a while. Blake threatened to hurt me if I didn't leave you alone. I'm taller and stronger than he is, but I felt I should avoid friction because I didn't want him to take out his anger on you." He waits.

Tali's crying and says, "I'm so sorry, little brother. I should have known that Blake was up to something when you and I started drifting apart. I've missed you so much! I love you, Roman!"

"I love you too, more than you know, Sis," he says. They have an in-depth conversation about Blake's antics that drove Roman away from Tali.

"I'll be in town on break soon. Let's hang out and catch up at home in Mission Viejo. I know we can repair the damage that Blake caused in our relationship."

"Absolutely!" confirms Tali. "I'm looking forward to being with you and feeling the comfort of our family."

25

Not Surprised

After the call from Roman, Tali opens her journal.

Dear Josie...OMG! My little brother just called me! We've rarely spoken since I married Blake and only seen each other briefly on holidays at our parents' house. He said he's not surprised that I'm divorcing Blake. Blake threatened my little brother and told him to stay away from me! Blake's such a demon! On a side note, no one—family or friends—is surprised I'm divorcing Blake! How did I not see the signs that I was in a toxic relationship with a textbook narcissist? I know. I know. They wear a mask to fool everyone around them with their love bombing and hoovering...then the gaslighting...the constant gaslighting... I'm just so mad at myself for falling into Blake's trap! And, Josie, get this...Blake is trying to get me to go to his brother's

*house for their annual family gathering next weekend!
Why doesn't he get it that I'm done with him? It makes
me wonder if he's told his parents yet. Thomas knows
that I'm divorcing him. Does he actually think that he can
shut it down before they find out? Knowing his deceitful,
controlling nature, that's probably the case. I should bring
this notion up to Shannon next week. She'll have some
interesting insights to share, I'm sure.*

26

She Deserves Nothing

Blake is sitting at his desk in Monterey, pondering the divorce situation. He needs to finish a PowerPoint presentation for tomorrow morning's project progress meeting, but he's distracted, thinking about how to tear Tali apart. He says under his breath, "She deserves nothing." Then, he emails his forensic accountant and tells him which interest/discount rates to use in the projected cash flow calculations for the marital assets.

Pamela only recently informed him that his emails can be used as exhibits in divorce court. When this case goes to court, Jay will interrogate Blake and his accountant regarding the method used for the calculations.

Tali's forensic accountant has already advised her to only call and text when she needs to talk about financial matters because emails will become evidence. Tali complies with her expert witnesses' advice.

27

They Cannot Be Alone

Six months into the divorce process, Blake's still living in Monterey. Tali has removed all contact and will only talk to him with her attorney present.

One evening after work, Blake goes for a run on the beach. He stops after two miles to catch his breath and watches the waves roll into the shore. He looks up at the moon, lost in his thoughts. As he turns to resume his run, he accidentally bumps into another jogger. They both fall to the sand. Blake reaches to help her up when their eyes meet. There's a sadness in her eyes, barely seen in the glow of the moonlight.

"I'm sorry," Blake says, thinking she should have been looking where she was going.

She says, "No, it's my fault. I should have run out farther around you. You seemed lost in thought. I should have been more aware."

Blake says, "It's my fault. I should have looked before turning to continue my run."

They both smile and look at each other for a moment. Blake reaches out his hand and says, "Hi. I'm Blake Solace."

She accepts his hand and returns a firm handshake, "Nice to meet you, Blake Solace. I'm Hope Winters."

Blake holds her hand and says, "I know we're kind of sweaty from running, but we can cool off walking together. Maybe we can go to a beach bar for a nightcap?"

Hope blushes a bit as she says, "Sure. I guess so."

"Okay then," says Blake. "Let's walk." He begins a polite, superficial conversation by asking Hope what she does.

They walk a quarter mile to the first beach bar they see. They enter the establishment, where a guitarist sings everyone's favorite beach life tunes. The place is busy on a Friday evening. They sit at the bar and peruse the drink menu. She orders a tequila sunrise, and he orders a bourbon on the rocks. Their conversation is guarded on both sides—as each person, unbeknownst to the other, is currently going through a divorce, and each has some trust issues right now. The evening concludes about two hours later with a light kiss and an exchange of phone numbers. She heads in the direction where they bumped into each other.

Blake continues up the beach toward the condominium where he's lived since moving for his job. He won't shop for a place to buy. No new assets are supposed to enter the picture until the divorce is finalized. His mind wanders as he walks, thinking about the offshore investments he's hiding from Tali and her attorney. He and Jeff, his colleague at the firm in Newport Beach, invested portions of their paychecks into an offshore deal that has paid off quite well. No reason to tell Tali about it. She would get upset that he was being risky with their money. But, in his mind, the whole risk-return tradeoff can be futile or fun. And, in this case, boy, has it been fun!

Thinking about Hope, he wonders if he might have someone to share some of the payoff with. His mind travels to his unexpected meeting. *She's so pretty. And she seems sweet. I'm excited to get to know her better.* He arrives at his place and walks inside to get ready for bed.

28

I'll See You in Court

Jay coaches Tali on what to expect in the courtroom and how best to handle and defeat Blake. She must manage her reactions.

"A narcissist will implode if you ignore them in the courtroom. People with this personality disorder can't tolerate being ignored. Don't acknowledge Blake's presence at any time. You are his source of power, and if he doesn't get reactions from you, he will get flustered, likely angry. That's what we want."

"I wish I'd known this sooner."

"It's never too late to develop sound strategies for self-defense when you're around narcissists. They are everywhere. The more you know about them and yourself, the better prepared you will be."

"I can avoid eye contact, but I hope I don't get emotional."

"Be yourself but be guarded in the courtroom."

"This whole thing is making me a stronger woman, Jay. Thank you!"

29

Dad Says Things About You

LeeAnn Silver picks up the children, Ashley and Andrew, from school and takes them out for ice cream and to a beachside playground. While sitting on the swings, Andrew asks, "Mom, are you okay?"

LeeAnn looks at him and says, "Yes, dear, why do you ask?"

"Just 'cause," he says hesitantly. He continues, "While Dad and I were working in the yard yesterday, he was telling me that I shouldn't listen to you 'cause you're brain damaged. What does brain damaged mean? Are you?" He looks up at LeeAnn with questioning eyes.

She hugs him and says, "No, I'm not brain damaged. Brain damage can have a myriad of meanings and reasons, but no, I'm fine. I'll talk with your dad to see why he said that." She hugs him tighter.

He says, "Thanks, Mom. I thought I should listen to you. That's why I'm telling you what Dad said about you. Please don't tell him I told you. He told me not to tell you what he said or he would hurt me."

"I won't say anything to him. You can trust me. I love you," she says.

"I love you, too, Mom,"

Meanwhile, Ashley has been listening. She gets up from her swing and walks over to hug Andrew and LeeAnn. She says, "Dad has been saying the same things to me whenever we're out shopping or on those stupid evenings he calls 'daddy-daughter dates.' He's always complaining about you, Mom, and he tells me it's my duty to listen to him complain about you. Dad's so mean. Do we have to live with him?"

LeeAnn is holding both children tightly as she says, "I have a new friend, a lady named Tali, who I think might be able to help us figure out what to do. I think it's time to make some changes in our family."

Both children express their agreement as tears stream down their faces. It took all the courage these little children had to share their dad's comments about her, especially since he'd threatened to hurt them if they ever told their mom what he'd said about her. LeeAnn knows she has to do something, starting with a call to Tali.

30

Dear Josie...

Dear Josie...I met with Jay today. Wow! Sounds like I'm in for a battle with Blake! Pamela has shared with Jay some of the rages Blake has thrust upon her. Pamela is so fed up with Blake, but she will stick it out. I'm trying not to be afraid of Blake, but it's hard. I wake up every day with a fearful dread in the pit of my stomach. Like, what's Blake going to try to do to hurt me today? Sydney, Bentley, and Molly are trying to help me through this. Mamita is coming to visit me next week. I can't wait. I'm so ready to finish this chapter of my life and move on to happier times. I still wonder. How did I ever get involved with someone as mean and psychotic as Blake? I still have flashbacks to the days of trying to recover from the car wreck, and that night in the wheelchair accessible apartment only eight weeks after the wreck when Blake made me have sex with him.
I couldn't even walk since I was still non-weight-bearing on

my legs and my broken hips and pelvis were not yet healed. Oh Josie, it hurt so bad. Jay says that experience was marital rape and he will bring it up in court. Blake said to me, "Just lie still. This won't hurt." But it did. Real bad. I cried, but Blake didn't care.

31

Break the Wall

Tali wraps up an early appointment with a client and runs to her car to rush over to Shannon's office for her weekly mid-morning session. When she arrives, Shannon's admin, Amy, ushers her to the usual designated counseling room and indicates that Shannon will join her in a few minutes. Tali sits on the edge of the worn leather chair.

As Shannon enters the room and pulls up a side chair, it is evident she has a preset agenda for today. She quickly asks Tali for any material updates. Tali mentions that the divorce logistics are moving forward and that Blake now has hired an attorney. She adds that Blake has been fluctuating in his demeanor toward her, playing nicey-nicey, then turning hateful and back to nicey-nicey—sometimes within the span of thirty minutes.

Shannon then says, "As I mentioned last week, I want to pour into you an even deeper understanding of some aspects of narcissism so you can better understand and navigate both through the divorce and post-divorce. It will give you added confidence that you have made the best decision for your situation with Blake. And it will give you some radar to use in life, in general, should you ever enter the dating and married world again."

Tali grimaces at that last comment.

"Today, Shannon begins, "I want to make you aware of what actually may go on inside a narcissist's mind and why this may apply to Blake. The phrase I use is 'breaking the fifth wall'—a term I am borrowing from the world of acting. On a set in a theater or on television, there are typically only three walls comprising a back wall and two side walls. This is sort of like the dollhouse you had as a little girl. The fourth wall in a theater is open, so the audience can look in, as if from a transparent, soundproof plexiglass wall to watch what is going on. The script is typically written to portray that the actors are unaware that the audience is watching them. An actor breaks the fourth wall if and when his or her character steps out of the scene as if hitting a pause button and talks to the audience directly."

Tali interrupts, "I understand the concept, but how does this relate to Blake?"

Shannon responds, "The fifth wall is like another dimension. I like to use the analogy of the ceiling. A theater set typically has no ceiling, so lighting and other equipment can be utilized from above. But the term 'breaking the fifth wall' can be used where the actor talks about him or herself, perhaps in a 'look at me' bragging type of way, and the audience is then directly involved as a part of the cast in the production. That is, the audience has a formal role to play."

Tali breaks in again, "So am I a broken fifth wall for Blake?"

Shannon explains further, "Well...I also want to introduce you to another character in your real-world play. It is a voice that only Blake may know. Tali, have you ever felt that Blake cannot even hear your voice as you explain how the world may interpret his diatribes, actions, and nonverbal communication toward others?"

"Absolutely, really all the time," Tali says affirmatively.

"Well, that's probably because he can't hear you, as someone constantly has his ear. It is an inner voice—like noise–that is preventing him from hearing you while the inner voice tells him that no matter what, in any situation, he is always the best of the best and is never wrong and never at fault—the greatest of all time or G.O.A.T. It is always someone else's fault. Sound familiar?"

Tali nods.

"Blake's inner voice is ready to yell, scream, shriek into Blake's mind, as if Blake were a marionette. His inner voice drowns out every syllable of your voice or someone else's voice trying to reason with Blake. It has likely permanently broken the fifth wall, causing Blake to live in an alternate place that is very different from where you, I, and others live. A narcissist makes his or her own rules, and those rules can change at any time to suit the narcissist's agenda. You've mentioned that playing a board game with Blake is always chaotic because he changes the rules to win. Blake wears a mask as he pretends to conform mechanically to our world. Tali, this is likely Blake's world—the broken fifth wall. A world that neither one of us can enter or see."

Tali starts to sob and cannot stop.

After a few minutes, Shannon adds, "I want you to think back through this session and watch for signs of Blake's inner voice occurring over the next week. When you return, we will discuss why Blake is as he is. I know this is painful, but it can provide you with long-lasting peace and understanding as you go forward in your own life, Tali. A life you deserve."

Tali takes a deep breath and says, "Thanks, Shannon. Lots to think about. This whole NPD thing is deeper and darker than I ever imagined."

32

Is He Yelling at You?

Blake's in a conference room talking with an employee about some financial projections. They stare at Blake's laptop screen as he scrolls through the spreadsheet columns. "What's the formula in this cell and why doesn't it reference the Fed funds rate in A152?" Blake inquires.

The employee, Heather, replies, "Yesterday, you instructed me to use the rate in B152 instead since you said to run the model retro first, and we would later bring the new rates into the model. Have you changed your mind?"

Blake glares at her with a look of disbelief on his face. "Why would I tell you to use that rate? Come on now. Use your little head. I never said that," his voice escalating. "We have to get this model complete and out to inter-company investors by the end of the day. With the intricacies of these calculations, this model requires two hours to run, and then we have to test the results. Remember the last time we sent out a model with bugs in it?

I got reamed by management when it wasn't even my fault!" He's screaming at her. The conference room door is closed, but office workers outside the room hear Blake's rant.

Heather looks at him, stands up and says she'll make the changes and send the model to him in ten minutes.

"Where are you going?"

"I'm returning to my desk, Blake, to finish this task. The air in here is a little stifling right now. I'll text you in about ten minutes when I send the updated file." She walks out of the conference room.

Blake sits there seething. He texts Hope, "I can't believe the disrespect I get around here! I'm the smartest person in this company! No one seems to recognize that fact!" He waits.

Hope replies, "Oh, I know. I know. You're the best. Everything will be okay. How about I run by the market on the way home from work and cook dinner for you tonight? xoxo"

He replies, "Thanks, babe. Sounds good. Look forward to it. Now, I better ensure my direct reports are doing the calculations correctly. Man, what a day. I hate my job. C u later xoxo." He picks up his laptop and exits the conference room.

Everyone in the office ignores him as he returns to his desk. As he walks past, he notices that Heather is in his boss' office with the door shut. She's sharing her experience. Blake's boss is keeping a log of his erratic behaviors.

Later that day, Blake and Hope have dinner at his extended-stay hotel. He hasn't purchased a place in Monterey since it looks like Tali will not be moving to Monterey anytime soon. He's still thinking that he can make her drop the divorce and repair their relationship.

In the meantime, he has Hope in his life. *She's a nice lady,* he thinks to himself as he looks at her across the dinner table.

She looks up and says, "What? Is there something wrong with me? You're staring at me. Is there spinach stuck in my teeth?"

"No, babe," he says. "I'm just admiring you. You're beautiful."

"Aw," she says. "Thanks. You're pretty cute yourself."

He says, "Ya, I am, aren't I? Bet you're glad I'm a runner too, or else we wouldn't have crossed paths on the beach that night."

She looks at him, thinking, *He's a bit conceited, but he is cute. Oh well. We'll see where this thing goes.*

He convinces her to spend the night even though she has an 8:00 a.m. call with an international law client in the morning. They finish dinner, and he tells her to help clean the kitchen. While she's loading the dishwasher, Blake's cell rings. He's gone out to his car to get something. Hope answers the call. It's Tali. The two ladies are talking when Blake returns to the kitchen.

"Who are you talking to? Is that my phone?" his voice escalates.

Hope says, "Tali, here he is," as she hands the phone to Blake. Blake grabs the phone out of her hand and screams, "Don't ever touch my phone again!" He then speaks into the phone, softening his tone, "Hi honey, what's up?"

Tali says, "Jay says we need to decide when to put the condo on the market. I'm willing to buy you out on your half, but if you're dead set on selling it, that's okay with me. I have my eye on another property near Molly's place. Your thoughts?"

By this time, Blake is seething with anger and says, "Really? You're still going through with the whole divorce thing? I'm coming down there next weekend so that we can hash this out, Tali. You're not leaving me!" he screams.

Hope listens to this conversation as she puts on her shoes and picks up her purse and keys. She quietly exits Blake's place and walks hurriedly to her car. While still on the phone, Blake glances out the window to see Hope driving away. *Damn,* he thinks. *These two women don't know what a prize I am.*

33

Hope Leaves Blake

Blake calls Hope after he finishes talking with Tali. She doesn't pick up his call, so he leaves a voicemail. Then, he texts her.

"Hey babe. Are you okay? Why did you leave?"

"You were screaming at her. You scare me. It's over."

He texts, "I didn't mean to scare you. Tali's a bitch. I was trying to make her see that I was right."

"Well, it sounded like you want her back."

"No, babe. I'm just wearing her down. I want you in my life. I'll make it up to you."

"I don't know. You sounded very mad. It was scary listening to you."

"How about we drive to San Fran this weekend? It's on me. We need some alone time together."

"I guess. Let me see how work goes this week. Good night."

"I'll make the hotel reservations. I know a fantastic place near the bay that you'll love xoxo."

Hope's work project intensifies as the week progresses, and she tells Blake that she cannot go to San Fran with him this weekend. He rages at her. She tells him this relationship is over.

He decides to let it go for now. He keeps the reservation and drives to San Francisco on Friday after work.

That weekend, Tali logged into their joint credit card app to review expenses—hers and his. She noticed a charge of $600 in San Francisco from the previous night. Then she reviews the charges for the last two months and adds up Blake's spending on new clothes: $7,000. *What's going on?* she wonders. She screenshots the charges and forwards them to Jay.

34

Let's Go

Saturday morning, Molly drives to Tali's place. Jasper and Misty excitedly greet Molly as she walks into the mud room.

"Hi!" says Molly.

Tali replies, "Hey there! I'll be right down." Tali walks downstairs into the kitchen and gives Molly a big hug. "I'm so excited to hang out on Catalina today," she says. "I haven't been to the island since the car wreck."

"Me too," says Molly. "I've been so busy with work that I haven't been there either. I heard there's a new café that's good. Wanna try it out for lunch?"

"Sure!" says Tali. They check on the water bowls for the pets, lock the doors, and start walking to the ferry dock. They arrive about thirty minutes before the boarding begins. They find seats on the stern atop the cushioned life preserver bin. The voyage will last about ninety minutes. They enjoy watching the dolphins swimming and breaking the surface along the way.

Upon entering the Catalina Island harbor, they each take a deep breath and sigh in wonderment at the beautiful setting and the yachts moored in the clear turquoise water. When the ferry docks and is secured, the passengers disembark for an island adventure. Tali and Molly begin walking into Avalon, stopping at little shops along the way. They inquire about the location of the new café and head in that direction. Upon arriving, the hostess seats them at an outdoor table near the water. Molly looks at Tali and says, "Okay, now this is a great idea! I need this day away, and I know you do, too."

Tali says, "Yes, I definitely need this. Thanks for coming here with me. I know you've been so busy with work."

"I want to be here for you. Now, fill me in on everything that's going on. Is Blake still dating? What's her name? Hope, is it?"

"I don't think so," Tali replies. "I'm not sure. His credit card charges have been inconsistent with those of a few weeks ago. In the past month, he spent $600 in one night in San Francisco and $7,000 on new clothes. Either he's shopping to try to look good on the outside or he's with someone he's trying to impress. I took a screenshot of his expenses and sent them to Jay. I don't know what's going through Blake's mind. He's been texting me daily to persuade me to meet with him and talk. I just can't be alone with him. He scares me."

"Aw," says Molly. "You're surrounded by your tribe, my friend. Don't be afraid of Blake. He can't hurt you anymore. But I get it. It's difficult to move on when a narcissist has abused you. I'm so sorry you're going through this, Tali." Molly reaches for Tali's hand.

Tali smiles and says, "I'm so thankful for you. And I'm thankful for my friends and family and Jay helping me traverse this chasm of narcissistic chaos. It's interesting. Shannon has taught me so much about how narcissists think and behave, and she's taught me how to respond and not react to Blake's words and antics. Wow, Molly. I want to get through this whole messy experience and move on with my life. Maybe I can do something to help people someday. Maybe I'll write a book to share some insights I've learned. No one should ever have to experience narcissistic abuse. It's so sad that there are people in this world like Blake."

Molly looks at Tali with concern and admiration. "I'm so proud of you for working with Shannon and Jay to figure out what to do. You need to focus on yourself and your healing. Don't rush the recovery. There will be time in the future to help others. Let's get you through this and help you heal from the abuse. I'm so sorry, babe. You deserve to be happy."

Tali smiles as she says, "Thanks. You and Chad are an amazing couple! You're so blessed to have each other. I hope I can be happy—like truly happy one day. Not fake happy the way I've been with Blake."

"You will be. I'm sure of that. Just don't rush it. God has someone for you, my friend. All in His timing."

Tali smiles and looks out to the horizon as she takes a deep breath. The two ladies finish their lunch and then spend the day walking around Avalon. They tour the casino and then walk to a beach bar for light cocktails and calamari. Around 4:00 p.m., they head toward the dock and board the ferry back to Newport Beach.

35

In Blake's Mind...

"Hey bro, what's up?" Thomas says, answering Blake's call.

"OMG!" Blake is hyper. His voice is tight and high-pitched. "Tali's causing me no end of problems! Why did I ever marry that bitch? I need to reel her back in. She's acting all high and mighty with her expensive attorney and trying to call the shots on this divorce thing that she started. Not my idea. We were fine. I still don't know why she's trying to leave me. I'm the best husband she could ever find!"

"What's happening with Hope?" interrupts Thomas.

"She blew me off. Everything feels tangled in knots. That's okay; having two women in my life was crazy. I'm just playing my cards close to the vest, waiting for Tali to crash and burn. And take my word, she will. Just wait for it."

Thomas hesitates after Blake finishes talking. "Okay then, little brother. It sounds like you've got it under control. What can I do to help?"

"I'm thinking about that," says Blake, "I'll let you know." They say their goodbyes and end the call.

36

The Angel

As Tali walks with Jasper on the beach, her thoughts churn. She seems to have as many thoughts as there are grains of sand lapped by the waves.

She's grateful Jay's been coaching her on how to handle a narcissist in the courtroom if they go to court...and it looks like they might, based on Blake's recent comments. He wants to go to court. She looks beyond the waves to the horizon. *What's on my horizon?* she wonders.

She suddenly feels a presence, something familiar, and instantly remembers having the same feeling when her car plummeted off the Pacific Coast Highway onto the rocks below. She turns around and notices a figure walking toward her and Jasper. There's something so familiar about him. He's tall, with salt-and-pepper hair and an athletic build. He has a smile on his face as he approaches Tali.

Jasper's wagging her tail and smiling the way a dog smiles. Tali's a bit guarded. It's 7:00 a.m. and there aren't many beach walkers this morning. Tia's café is nearby if she needs to run away.

Well, she thinks to herself, *I can't run as fast as I used to before I got metal implants in my leg.* She's had to endure a lot of surgical repairs even to be walking. *And why isn't Jasper barking?* She smiles a little as the man walks over to them.

"May I pet your dog? She looks so sweet!" he says.

"Sure. I guess," she replies. The man bends down to pet Jasper, who gets so excited that she licks his face with her big, slobbery tongue.

"Oh no, Jasper, down. I'm so sorry," says Tali.

"It's okay," he says. "I love dogs. I had a golden retriever once. They're very social animals!" He continues to pet Jasper.

Tali smiles as she says, "I'm glad you understand. Are you from around here?" She's trying to figure out in her mind why he seems familiar to her. Maybe she met him at a previous interior design job? She's thinking.

"Kinda," he says.

"What does that mean?" she asks.

"Well, I tend to go where I'm needed. I've been here a few times. I've also worked a few jobs further up the Pacific Coast Highway." He looks up at her as he pets Jasper's head.

Tali looks into his eyes, wondering why he's being so vague, and decides she doesn't want to trust him. She pulls Jasper away from him.

He says, "Tali, I'm not here to alarm you. I just came here to check on you."

"How do you know my name? Did Blake send you to spy on me?" she asks as she turns to start briskly walking toward Tia's café.

He reaches for her shoulder.

Shuddering, she pulls away from him, but she stops in her tracks when he says, "My name's Aaron. I was there with you when your car went over the cliff and hit the rocks on the shore below. I stayed with you and told you to breathe while we waited for the first responders to arrive. I was with you on the air ambulance, and I stayed in the hospital with you. I was in the hospital room with you all those times when no one else was there, including Blake. I went to the rehabilitation hospital with you. You couldn't see me all those times, but I was there with you. God instructed me to watch over you. He told me you've been questioning your spiritual path lately due to Blake's antics and this divorce. I'm just here to check on you and reassure you that everything will be okay."

She stands there with tears streaming down her face, trying to speak, but she cannot. Finally, she says, "It's you. You were there. No one else saw you. I asked the police to find you. They never could. They said that no one else besides the police and fire rescuers was there that night by my car. But you were there. Why couldn't they see you?"

"Because my job is to be your guardian angel, Tali. God blessed me with this mission, and I love it! You're one of the most adventuresome people I've ever been assigned!"

Tali smiles a bit through the tears as she says, "Sorry about that. I know...the college days...Bentley's bungee jumping...I'm really sorry about that..." she trails off.

He says, "I'm honored to be your angel. Again, my name's Aaron." He reaches to shake her hand.

She accepts the gesture and shakes his outreached hand. "Well, obviously, you know my name. This pup is Jasper, and she obviously likes you a lot. They say dogs have a sixth sense about people. I guess you're a person. Are you human?"

"I look human to you, but I'm of the spiritual realm. People and living organisms, like Jasper here, can only see me when they're supposed to see me. For example, you were supposed to hear my voice to help comfort you after your car wreck, but you and everyone else were not supposed to see me after that. But, as I shared earlier, I was there with you during your entire recovery. Now, I'm back to help you walk through this divorce journey, so you know that God is with you and everything will be okay. You're not going to lose everything. You're not going to be living under a bridge somewhere."

She looks quizzically at him.

He adds, "God shared some insights into your recent internal questions so that I could figure out what to say and do to reassure you right now." He continues petting Jasper and waits for Tali to process everything he's said.

She looks out at the ocean and says, "Aaron, thank you for telling me. This is a lot to think about. Since the wreck, I've wondered if I had only imagined hearing your voice that night. I just chalked it up to shock and delusion. I was pretty injured. It's taken time to heal from the injuries and surgeries physically, and I'm still not where I want to be. One thing is sure: I'll never take being able to walk for granted."

He says, "I'm so happy to hear you say that. You're a gift to so many people, Tali, with your spirit of perseverance and gratitude for the blessings in your life. You have no idea how many lives you touch in such a positive way each day." He smiles at her.

"Thanks, I needed to hear that. I've been pretty beaten down and broken while being married to Blake. I'm just trying to muddle through each day during this divorce while maintaining professionalism and composure at my job. It's tough. Walking on the beach with my pup has helped me clear my mind and get through another day. And my family and friends in my tribe. I couldn't make it through this life without them. It's just so hard trying to battle Blake. Now that I'm aware of how evil and controlling he's always been, it's hard to trust myself, let alone anyone else." She pauses, adding, "Thanks for letting me know you're here for me and that God knows my struggles."

Aaron says, "You're so welcome, Tali." He stands up and reaches to pat her on the shoulder. She asks him for a hug if that's allowed.

"Of course." He hugs her, saying, "I'm always here with you."

They embrace as the waves crash into the shore and the seagulls call out to each other. Then he is gone. She's standing there with Jasper, wondering if she just imagined the whole thing...him. Then, with her highly tuned instincts, she knows he was real. She smiles as she and Jasper walk up the beach toward the townhouse so she can get ready for work. She thinks, *What a beautiful start to a new day.*

37

Prove It!

Shannon and Tali are deep in a therapy session when Shannon tells her more about being with a narcissist.

"When you fear a narcissist, you always believe that you have to prove yourself to them—prove that you are worth loving. Research shows evidence of this phenomenon in children of narcissists. Trying to earn the love of a narcissist is futile."

Tali is reminded of the time Blake fired the housekeeper while Tali was in the hospital. Then he made Tali do all of the townhouse chores when she could barely walk and was still recovering from the car wreck.

"I thought I could do and be everything he wanted me to be. I lost any idea of who I was. It was about reflecting on him, making him feel good about himself. I did that so he would be good to me."

"You've learned an awful lot the hard way. How do you feel about yourself now?"

"I think I'm only beginning to find out who I really am, and that feels good," Tali says thoughtfully.

"That, my dear, is what it's all about."

38

Getting Ready for Court

"Thanks, Jay, for coaching me on how to handle a narcissist in the courtroom, especially since I haven't handled one very well in real life."

"You'll be ready," Jay says.

Tali is very anxious about going to court, knowing it will be a battle.

"First," Jay says, "deflate him by ignoring him. Make him feel irrelevant. That will cause a narcissist to implode right in front of you. I had a client whose narcissistic husband faked his wife's resume and gave it to an expert witness. The resume was all incorrect—job titles, company names, and dates of employment were all wrong. When the expert witness interviewed the wife, she questioned where he obtained the document. He said that the husband's attorney gave it to him. The wife edited the faked resume in red, and both documents became exhibits in the court case, along with eighty-nine other exhibits."

Tali looked at him. "Eighty-nine?"

"True story. When the judge heard about what the narcissistic husband was saying and doing during a conversation with the two attorneys, he said that he didn't want that asshole in his courtroom and to mediate the divorce case. They did, and the wife won, of course." He continued, saying, "I just want to assure you that we are in good shape to overturn Blake's suppositions and accusations."

Tali feels hopeful. Or does she? Tali's been researching ways to defeat a narcissist in court. Can a narcissist be defeated? Yes! She's creating a matrix of strategies to address—or instead, ignore him—by becoming a "gray rock." She rehearses Jay's words: redirect, reject, refocus, record, repurpose.

39

Real Scars

Dear Josie...I have so many scars from the car wreck and surgeries...am I still pretty? I remember Blake telling me to wear make-up while I was still bandaged and living in a wheelchair. He told me I had to wear makeup so I'd look prettier. He's so cruel. Words can hurt, and words can heal. His words hurt me.

If only I'd paid attention to my daddy's whispered comment while walking me down the aisle on my wedding day. He and Mamita, and Roman, knew that I was marrying someone who wasn't right for me. But I was so stubborn. I thought I was in love. What was I thinking? Daddy whispered to me halfway down the aisle, "Peaches, we can turn around right now and go home if you want." I whispered back, "No, Daddy. I love him." And we walked down the aisle toward Blake, the man who would become my arch nemesis. I didn't realize it at the time. I was already a victim of Blake's love bombing me campaign... soon followed with gaslighting...more rages...flying monkeys...even more rages...hoovering...more gaslighting... and the vicious cycle continued into today. The struggle is real. The scars are real—both the visible and invisible.

40

In His Head

Blake's sitting at his desk with his back to the doorway, looking out the window, when his boss enters his workspace.

"Hey Blake, you got a minute?"

"Sure. What's up?"

His boss sits down and hands Blake a file. "I want you to review this carefully. It's your recent 360-degree performance review. The bottom line is that your coworkers, managers, and direct reports state that you need improvement—that you're inflexible, don't listen, must have your way, and that you micromanage. Out of curiosity, I called one of my colleagues at your previous employer in Newport Beach this morning."

Blake says, "Oh, you did?"

"Yes. I've been informed that you had very similar issues at your old firm. I need to figure out what's up with you, Blake. I scheduled an appointment this afternoon with you and a coach in the human resource department who specializes in this type of situation."

"Oh, now I'm a situation?" Blake says with a slight escalation in tone and volume.

"Now, don't get defensive. I think Sheila can help you work through some of the rough spots in your management style."

"Oh great, a female named Sheila is going to help me. I can already tell you that this will be a total waste of time for everyone. Are you serious?"

"Yes, I'm serious. I have a file on you, Blake. You are smart but replaceable if you're unwilling to work on these personality matters hindering your management development. Give Sheila and her coaching process a chance." He stands up to leave. "And know this...you don't have another choice. Well, except to quit. I don't think you want to do that while going through a divorce—right?"

Blake looks up at him. "How'd you know about the divorce?"

"Oh, I know way more than anyone realizes. The boss has to keep an ear to the ground to know what's going on in the lives of his people." He smiles and leaves the room.

Blake's furious. *Another "needs improvement" job performance review. I'm not inflexible. I don't micromanage. I just know the best way to get things done. If it's going to be done right, it has to be done my way. This Sheila won't know what hit her.*

41

Let It Unfold

After work, Tali and Jasper head to the beach. As Tali watches the waves rolling into shore, she begins to pray. *Oh God, how can I do this? I know...I know...you've outfitted me with the tools and people to effectively battle Blake at his own game. And thanks for Aaron, by the way. I'm sorry, but I'm still feeling weak. I'm afraid of what Blake will do to me in the courtroom.* Tali suddenly feels like a question is arising in her subconscious spirit... like God is saying to her, "Trust Me...do you trust Me?"

Tali's phone buzzes, and she returns to reality from her meditative state. She answers, "Hello?"

LeeAnn says, "Hi Tali! It's LeeAnn, Gordon's wife. I'd like to follow up on something you said when I ran into you and your mother at the yacht club."

"Hi, LeeAnn. How are you?"

"Actually, not great. I need to talk. Are you busy?"

"Just walking my dog on the beach right now. But I'm happy to get together or talk on the phone."

LeeAnn replies, "Could we meet for dinner this evening? The children are spending the night at my parents' place."

"Sure thing," Tali says. "Let me get back to the townhouse and feed the pets. Do you want to come to my place? We can order takeout."

"That sounds lovely," says LeeAnn. "What time and what's the address?"

"Around seven would be great. I'll text you the address."

"Thanks Tali. See you soon."

The two ladies ended the call. Tali texts LeeAnn her address. Then, she and Jasper turn around to head back to the townhouse. Upon arriving, Misty saunters to Tali, purring and nudging her food dish. Tali pats Misty on her side, saying, "Oh dear, your tummy must be hungry. I guess Jasper and I walked a little longer than usual. Sorry about that, little girl. Here, let me fill your food dish. I'll give you some leftover sushi after dinner tonight."

Misty looks up at her as if she understands and nudges Tali's leg with her tail. Tali feeds both pets and fills their water bowls, then walks into the kitchen to fill her glass with cold water from the fridge.

She looks at the oven clock. It's 6:30 p.m. She climbs the stairs to freshen up a bit before LeeAnn arrives. Promptly at 7:00, the doorbell chimes. Jasper runs to the door, with Tali following closely behind. As she opens the door, Jasper sits at Tali's command, and LeeAnn bends down to pat Jasper's head. Jasper's tail wags as she graciously accepts this new visitor into their home. Tali is continually amazed at how Jasper knows whether a person has good intentions. Jasper knew Aaron was a good guy when they crossed paths on the beach a few days ago. It's that sixth sense.

The two ladies hug and then walk through the foyer into the kitchen. Tali says, "Would you like something to drink? I have a nice Sauvignon Blanc, cheese, fruit, and crackers while we decide what to order for dinner."

LeeAnn replies, "That sounds nice. Thanks so much for letting me come over on such short notice. I need to talk about some disturbing news my children recently shared. Like I said earlier, they're staying with my parents until I can figure some stuff out."

Tali pours two glasses of wine and puts cheeses, grapes, strawberries, and crackers on a tray. While she gets plates, napkins, and utensils out of the cabinet, she says, "Let's sit on the terrace while we talk." LeeAnn agrees and helps Tali bring the beverages and snacks outside.

When settled at the table, Tali says, "Now tell me what's happening. What did your children say that makes you so concerned?"

LeeAnn begins, "While we were at the playground after school the other day, Ashley and Andrew were telling me the things Gordon has been saying about me to them. They started crying. It was all lies. He uses the excuse of wanting daddy-daughter dates and father-son trips to work on brainwashing them and turning them against me." She waits a few seconds and looks up at the sky, tears welling up in her eyes. She continues, "He's always putting guilt trips on me if I don't get all the laundry or dishes done. I work full-time and take care of the children. I'm trying." Tears are streaming down her face at this point. "I didn't know where to turn, but then I remembered you and your mom, and you mentioned being in the middle of divorcing a narcissist. I know you're busy with work and the divorce. On top of that, Gordon is one of your interior design clients. I don't want to put you in a bad spot."

Tali says, "Oh, LeeAnn, it's okay. Let's consider what we can do to help you and your children. I have a few questions. First, does Gordon yell at you and the children?"

LeeAnn replies, "Yes, he does. Practically every day. The children are afraid of him. I'm afraid of him. The children's friends are afraid of him. Their friends have stopped coming over for playdates if they know Gordon's home."

"Does he blame you or the children for situations he caused? For example, didn't he demand that you bring his credit card to the yacht club that day and that you were to blame that his card was not in his wallet when he was the one who left it on his nightstand because he was ordering pocket squares the previous night?"

LeeAnn says, "Yes. You've got quite the memory, Tali. He yelled at me at the yacht club the day you and your mom had lunch. He constantly claims that all mishaps are my fault. Sometimes it is my fault, like he yelled at me for spilling the taco meat one evening while I was putting leftovers away after dinner. He didn't need to yell at me. The children saw the whole thing. He's a loose cannon. We're afraid he's going to hurt us."

Tali says, "He's already done that, my dear. He's hurting you and the children with his rages and accusations and lies and brainwashing tactics. I'm sorry that you're going through this, LeeAnn." Tali touches her hand to try to console her.

LeeAnn holds Tali's hand as she tries to regain her composure. She looks out at the ocean and thinks about what to say next. She turns back to face Tali. "I just don't know what to do. My parents and family have watched Gordon gradually suck the life out of me over the past ten years. They're deeply concerned. Now that the children have come to me with the lies that Gordon has told them, I am even more concerned. I guess I've just always tried to buffer his tantrums and harshness. When we married, I thought I could help Gordon gain confidence since his family didn't believe in him. His older brothers bullied him, and his parents always took their side, or so he said. Maybe he was also lying about his childhood. I don't believe a word he says to me anymore, and I don't trust him. I don't know what to do, except that I must protect my children from further damage from him. My parents are stepping in to help me. Gordon's out of town on business for a few days, so I'm trying to figure out a way to handle this situation before he returns."

Tali's thinking as she says, "You're doing the right thing with your parents taking care of your children while you sort this out. I'm not telling you what to do. I know firsthand what it's like to have a narcissistic husband yelling at you every day and always telling you what to do. So please know that I'm not directing you in any way. I've been listening to you, and I agree that you need to do something to protect your children from their dad, and you need to protect yourself. That's hard. My narcissist husband—soon to be ex-husband, I hope, after the impending court date next week—actually physically abused me, as well as mentally and emotionally. I'm not asking you to share more details about what Gordon's done to you or the children, but I want you to know I can relate. I don't ever say that I understand because we all travel different journeys, but I can relate to what you say you've experienced."

"Thanks, Tali," LeeAnn says quietly.

Tali continues, "I have two recommendations for you: First is my awesome therapist, and second is my best-of-the-best family law attorney. With your permission, I'll share your contact information with them, so they'll recognize your call if you reach out to them."

LeeAnn says, "Thank you so much. You're truly a gift from God in my life, Tali. What would I do now if I hadn't crossed paths with you at the club?"

Tali squeezes her hand and says, "God's got you. Just let this whole thing unfold. It's His plan and the right time will come. You and your children are going to be okay."

LeeAnn tries to smile, but her expression reveals her doubt.

"Now then, my new friend, let's order dinner! I promised my cat, Misty, some leftover sushi. Are you good with ordering sushi for dinner? If not, we can order something else."

LeeAnn says, "Sushi sounds wonderful!" The two ladies laugh as they gather the dishes and snack tray off the terrace table and walk back inside. Tali grabs her phone to look up her favorite sushi place's number and menu. They make their selections and place the order. The expected delivery is forty-five minutes. While they wait, Tali and LeeAnn walk upstairs to Tali's art studio to look at Tali's recent ocean sketches. LeeAnn shares some ideas on color and technique that Tali had never considered. Tali and LeeAnn are both feeling grateful for a new friendship in the art world—and in the world of surviving narcissistic abuse.

42

No Coincidences

A few days later, Tali and LeeAnn are walking Jasper on the beach. They've stayed in touch since LeeAnn revealed her concerns about her husband.

They walk silently, and then LeeAnn asks, "Do you believe in God?"

Tali responds, "Yes, I do. God has helped me figure some things out while I've been married to Blake." She thinks about Aaron, her guardian angel, but decides to save that for a later conversation.

LeeAnn then asks, "But how do you know when God's leading you, Tali?"

She replies, "It's just a feeling, I guess. Then, things start coming together differently than you imagined, like coincidences suddenly becoming clearer about how and when they happened. Like you and I meeting as if it were happenstance at the yacht club. Do you think that was a coincidence? Think about the timing. Your children are opening up to you, and I 'happen' to be dealing with a similar type of spouse's personality disorder in my marriage. I don't think it was a coincidence. Do you?"

LeeAnn stops walking and looks at the waves, saying, "No. That was not a coincidence. You and I were supposed to cross paths. Gordon demanded that I come down to the club to bring his credit card when I had an important meeting at the museum. I had no idea I would meet you." LeeAnn begins to cry.

Tali touches her shoulder and says, "It's okay. Just let it go. I'm sorry. These won't be the last tears you shed over Gordon. Let each day and each experience unfold as it should—God's in control. A lesson I have learned recently is that God doesn't bring you this far through a situation and then leave you. Allow Him to travel this journey with you. There are times when you'll feel so downtrodden that you'll be crying out, asking God to carry you because you feel like you cannot take another step—physically, mentally, or emotionally."

They stop walking, and LeeAnn looks at Tali. "How do you do it?"

"Let's walk over to Tia's Café to sit and talk. It's one of my go-to places, especially on rough days. You'll love Tia. She's a breath of fresh air! And her cuisine is to die for!"

"Sounds amazing! I'm starved!" LeeAnn says. The ladies laugh and head back up the beach.

43

Days Before

The following day, Jay calls Tali. "Do you know where Blake is?" he asks. "Pamela is looking for him. There are some disclosure documents that he needs to sign before we enter the courtroom on Friday."

"I haven't heard from him since last week," Tali says. "It's been nice."

Jay says, "I realize it's been more peaceful without him blowing up your phone with his hoovering, but we have to find him or file a Court Order. I'll start the Court Motion process this morning, which is the first step. He'll have until tomorrow morning to respond or be in contempt. Pamela agrees with me. Blake has been AWOL since last Friday. He won't return her texts or calls."

"Oh wow," Tali says. "Is it common for the respondent in a divorce case to disappear?"

Jay replies, "It's more common than you'd imagine. Especially when the respondent is a narcissist. They are typically very puzzled as to why anyone would divorce them in the first place because they believe that they've done nothing wrong. It's sad. Really. My assistant, Mallory, is currently drawing up the Court Motion paperwork. I'll file it with the court this morning. Let me know if Blake contacts you, and I'll do the same. Hang in there, Tali. We've got this covered."

They say their goodbyes and end the call. Tali sits at her desk for a few moments, pondering the conversation.

Sydney passes Tali's open office door and sees her staring out the window. "Hey girl," Sydney says. "Everything okay?"

Tali sighs and says, "I guess. Blake is nowhere to be found, and Jay says there are documents he must sign before our court date on Friday. What does he think he's doing? He's always delaying the divorce process. Why can't he go along with this? I heard that his girlfriend, Hope, left him. I'm ready to be done with Blake Solace!"

Sydney says, "I know you are. Let me know what I can do to help you."

"Thanks. Just listening to me go on about his antics is a true blessing. Thanks, boss."

"Anytime, dear," Sydney says and smiles as she turns to leave. Then, she turns back around and says, "By the way, Gordon Silvers likes the changes you made to the yacht club designs. He says he wants us to visit the club for lunch tomorrow to look at his boat. He wants to redo some interior work in his galley and two staterooms. From what I understand, it's a ninety-six-foot sailboat. Should be an interesting design opportunity."

"Interesting," says Tali. "Seems like opportunities to interact with narcissists keep popping up everywhere."

"I can ask someone else to handle the boat job if you want," says Sydney.

"It's okay. I'll do it since he's asking for me. He is very difficult. I'm glad you'll see the boat with me tomorrow. I don't like to be alone with Gordon. He's a bit creepy."

Sydney says, "I'm sorry, Tali. How about this idea? You're almost done with the yacht club space redesign. Let's team up on the boat job. Might be fun." She looks inquisitively at Tali.

"I'd love that!" Tali says.

"Okay then. I'll call Gordon to schedule our meeting tomorrow," Sydney says, walking away.

Tali walks over to her drafting table as her cell buzzes. It's a text from Blake.

She texts back. "Where are you?"

'I'm in San Francisco today. Thinking about you. I miss you. Can't we reconcile? Life's not worth living without you."

She screenshots the messages as his texts come through and forwards them to Jay. Jay texts her back, saying he's forwarding the messages to Pamela so she can contact him about the Court Motion.

Tali returns to Blake's texts, which come one after another. *This is like drinking from a firehose*, Tali thinks to herself. *I'm so done. Court on Friday. Let's see how that goes. If Blake even shows up.*

A few hours later, Jay calls Tali to report that Pamela received the e-signed documents she needed from Blake. "She says Blake will arrive in Newport Beach Thursday evening to meet with her to prepare for the Friday morning court date."

"I'm still skeptical that Blake's lying and that he'll try to pull some shenanigans before Friday."

Jay tries to reassure her. They ended the call with plans to meet Thursday morning for a final coaching session before the day in court.

The week progresses, with Tali and Sydney meeting with Gordon to discuss final sign off on the yacht club designs and a tour of his yacht. Tali's thankful that Sydney is teaming up with her on this project. She keeps thinking about how narcissists are entering her hemisphere. *They're everywhere.*

Thursday morning, Tali and Jasper walk to the beach. It's a quiet morning. Still early. The seagulls fly overhead as the sun begins to illuminate the seascape. Tali's reflecting on her conversation with Jay in preparation for tomorrow's court experience. She's feeling anxious. She looks to the horizon and remembers something Mamita shared with her as a little girl. Mamita taught her about Ephesians 6, which explains God's Armor. Tali closes her eyes while trying to recall the Bible lesson. *Let's see,* she thinks. *God, please dress me in your helmet of salvation. Your breastplate of justice. Your belt of truth. Your footgear of the zeal to spread your word and gospel. Please help me carry your shield of faith and the sword of your word and spirit.* She stands there in silence while Jasper chases a sand crab. Opening her eyes, she feels a sudden rush of peacefulness throughout her body. She feels more confident. She and Jasper walk a bit further up the beach before turning around to head home. Tali's thinking about tomorrow. *I feel more ready. Let's see what tips Jay shares during this morning's coaching session.*

Upon arriving at Jay's office, Mallory greets Tali and walks her back to Jay's office.

"Hi Tali! How are you?"

Tali replies, "Hi, Jay. Good. I guess."

"Okay, let's get started." He picks up a stack of legal pads and flips through the pages to show her the line of questioning that he's designed for the court encounter with Blake. He shares the questions that he'll pose to Blake. Tali is impressed with his organization and depth of the interrogation he's planned for Blake. Tali previously reviewed the sixty-eight exhibits Jay and his team put together, which will be discussed in court tomorrow, and the twelve exhibits Blake's attorney sent over.

Jay tells Tali that he knows Blake's antics during her recovery from the car wreck were unconscionable and could bring up dormant emotions in Tali, but that he will question Blake about those activities.

Tali agrees that's the right thing to do. "I'll do my best to keep my emotions in check. No guarantees."

"You're allowed to request a timeout—or a ten-minute break—during court tomorrow if you need to go outside to get some fresh air. Being in a court battle with a narcissist can feel as if all of the air has been sucked out of the room. Remember to avoid eye contact with Blake. Make eye contact with the court assistant while taking the oath of truth. Then, only look at me and the judge. A narcissist gets very uncomfortable when made to feel irrelevant, so make no eye contact with Blake. He will probably begin to rage, but still don't acknowledge him."

Tali instinctively recorded Blake's rages on her smartphone a while back and played them for Jay. Jay tells her that those recordings might come up in court if needed.

She's staying at Molly's that night. With Blake coming her way, she doesn't want to be alone.

44

Day in Court:
Watch the Narcissist's Mask Slip

Tali wakes up to the aromas of fresh coffee and banana bread. She stretches and reaches over to pet Jasper and Misty.

Molly knocks on the door. "Good morning, sunshine!"

Tali replies, "Good morning! Come on in."

Molly opens the door and walks over to pet Jasper and Misty. Molly's kit and pup are on her heels, ready to greet their friends. The pets run out of the room and race down the stairs to go outside. Chad meets them in the kitchen and opens the back door. Molly and Tali talk briefly while Tali stretches a bit more, working old car wreck stiffness out of her bones. The two ladies walk downstairs to the kitchen. Chad pours them cups of freshly brewed coffee and pulls banana bread out of the oven.

"That smells so good," says Tali. "It was so nice of you to let me and the pets stay over last night."

Molly and Chad both say, "Of course. You have a big day in front of you."

Chad adds, "I've baked your favorite banana bread and cut up some fresh fruits. Let's all sit on the terrace for breakfast." Molly and Tali help Chad bring the dishes out to the terrace. They enjoy breakfast, watching the pets play in the backyard. While the ladies finish their meal, Chad enters to get water and food bowls for the kits and pups.

Tali says to Molly, "Wow. He's amazing. You two are so perfect together."

Molly replies, "Yep. He sure is. I'm blessed." She reaches out to hold Tali's hand for a moment. Tali looks out at the beach being illuminated as the sun rises. She knows today is a big day. What the outcome will be, she's not quite sure. But it will all be okay. She's grateful Jay recommended getting the pets registered as her emotional support animals, so she can get custody of them. She holds onto that thought while she finishes her coffee. The three of them bring the empty dishes back inside. Molly and Chad encourage Tali to get ready while they clean the kitchen and get the pets settled inside.

She gratefully agrees, and about an hour later, Tali leaves to go to the courthouse. She parks her car in the garage below the building and walks upstairs to the main floor. She and Jay had arranged to meet in a side room thirty minutes before court commences. He's there waiting for her. They talk and review his line of questions one more time. About twenty minutes later, they walk over to the courtroom entrance. They take their respective seats at the table in the front. Blake and Pamela have not yet arrived. Suddenly, there are voices behind them.

Blake is saying something to Pamela under his breath in a curt tone. Pamela looks upset.

Did Blake just rage at Pamela? Tali wonders.

Blake and Pamela take their seats at the other table in front. Next, Blake's two expert witnesses arrive in the courtroom. Tali's expert witness was already seated when she and Jay arrived. Jay glances over at Pamela with a concerned expression. He and Pamela are friends outside of the courtroom, and he feels sorry for her for having to work with Blake. Hopefully, today's court battle will end with a settlement decision.

Everyone in the room rises as the judge enters from his chambers. He takes his seat, and all return to their chairs. The two attorneys approach the bench at the judge's request for a consultation. He tells them that this hearing should result in a settlement by this afternoon, per his review of the case.

Jay and Pamela agree with the judge. They both know Blake will drag this out as long as he can. The two attorneys return to their seats. Since Tali is the petitioner in the case, Jay first explains her reasons for filing for divorce. He then shares the first set of exhibits. The judge listens intently and takes some notes as he examines the exhibits.

Next, Pamela stands to explain Blake's position as respondent in this case. She doesn't share any exhibits at this time. The judge listens to Pamela while observing Blake's facial expression and body language. Upon finishing her initial statement, Pamela takes her seat. Jay then calls Blake to the stand. After completing the oath of truth, Jay begins questioning Blake.

"Why are you and Mrs. Solace in this courtroom today, Mr. Solace?"

Blake replies, "For some reason, Tali wants a divorce. I don't know why. I've always been a great husband. I take care of everything."

"Please just answer the question," Jay says. He continues, "So she wants a divorce. Is your marriage troubled?"

Blake replies, "No. Not at all. Tali has some mental issues. She's delusional about our marriage having problems. No marriage is perfect."

Jay says, "I present this transcript from a recent email conversation, which Tali openly shared with me, as an exhibit in this case." He hands a copy of the transcript to the judge and Blake.

"Mr. Solace, please read this transcript out loud." Blake proceeds hesitantly to read the document.

"Please speak up," Jay says.

The color rises in Blake's face, and his eyes grow dark. His email to Tali threatened her if she continued the divorce process. The email was dated two weeks ago.

Tali purposefully didn't look at Blake but watched the judge's face as Blake read the document. The judge was taking notes on his copy of the exhibit.

Jay then says, "Mr. Solace. Did you attack Tali outside in the parking lot of a local restaurant twelve months ago?"

Blake replies, "No. I did not. She kicked me in the nuts. She attacked me."

Jay replies, "Here is the next exhibit. The police report from that evening." He hands a copy of the police report to the judge. Jay continues, "The report states that the restaurant management and staff witnessed you chasing Tali out of the restaurant and pressing her face against her car. She wrestled to get free, kicking you in self-defense before she drove away. The restaurant management and staff called the police because of what they saw. They said you'd run out of the building without paying the bill and were afraid of what you might do to them if you returned to the restaurant. Comments, Mr. Solace?"

At this point, Blake's face is brick red, and his eyes are as black as onyx. He's breathing loudly and trying to catch Tali's gaze. She looks intently at the legal pad on the table before her.

He takes a deep breath and replies, "Tali's not well. I was trying to calm her down. She attacked me when I was trying to help her. She was being very irrational that night, as she often is these days. I'm not sure what's wrong with her, but others have also noticed it."

Tali clenches her teeth as she listens to his lies but shows no outward signs of distress.

Jay continues with a change of subject. "Let's look at yours and Tali's household finances. You have each put together a representative Statement of Position and Statement of Income and Expenses. The two sets of documents are comparable. I have a question, though. The affidavits from your previous employer indicate that you and a colleague were investing in some offshore accounts. Also, looking at your joint bank account and paycheck deposits, there seem to be some discrepancies in the monies being deposited from your previous employer during your time of employment. Portions of later paycheck deposits going to an offshore account are omitted. Please explain this discrepancy, Mr. Solace."

Blake is squirming and staring at Pamela who is looking at her notes in preparation for her line of questioning. "I don't know what you're referring to," Blake says.

Jay presents a copy of the affidavit and bank statements to Blake and the judge.

"There must be some sort of mistake," Blake says. "This isn't right." His discomfort is evident as he stares hard at Pamela.

Pamela requests a ten-minute recess, which the judge approves. Blake quickly leaves the courtroom, heading for the front door. Pamela runs after him. "Blake, we need to talk."

"Not now. I need some air." They both step outside onto the front steps of the building.

"Okay, Blake. I'm representing you. Did you lie in that court-room?" Pamela asks.

"No. Of course not," Blake says.

"Well then. You'd better explain very clearly to the judge and all of us in that room exactly what Jay's talking about in that last question when we return to the courtroom."

"Okay! I'll explain! Just get out of my face!" he screams at Pamela. She turns to walk back inside the building. Blake stands outside for a few minutes, vigorously texting his old colleague, Jeff. Jeff does not respond. They were both involved in the offshore deals with company funds and with their pay-check funds. After a few minutes, he returns to the courtroom and resumes his place on the stand.

Jay stands to continue his line of questioning. "Mr. Solace, I will leave the question about offshore monies on the table for a moment. I want to move on to when a wrong-way driver hit Tali on the interstate." Blake's expression turns to one of slight concern as he looks at Tali. She still refuses to look at him. She's looking at the judge. Jay continues, "Tell us about your wife's injuries."

Blake hesitates and says, "It was bad. I thought she was go-ing to die. I couldn't lose her. I love her." He pretends to wipe a tear from his eye.

Jay says, "Do continue. What were her injuries? I have her hospital X-rays as evidence, but we want your description."

Pamela remains quiet. She knows where this is going.

"She had compound fractures in her arm and leg. She was bleeding internally, and the doctors couldn't stop the bleed-ing. Eventually, it stopped. Not sure how. I think her hips were broken. Oh yeah, and her pelvis was fractured. The sur-geons put metal plates there. Tali jokes about having buns of steel." He laughs shallowly. "It's been a while. Did I mention everything?"

"You mentioned enough. Not all. But enough. So, Mr. Solace, my next question to you is why did you make Tali have sex with you when she was still non-weight-bearing and confined to a wheelchair or bed with two broken hips and a broken pelvis, which had been re-enforced with metal plates after undergoing five of the nine surgeries that would ultimately be required to repair her injuries from the head-on collision?"

Everyone in the room gasps.

Blake is quiet as he looks over at Tali. The judge looks directly at Blake as she says, "Mr. Solace, we're waiting to hear your response."

With tears in his eyes, Blake begins with, "I don't know what to say. I love her. I thought she loved me. I just wanted to show her how much I loved her that night. It didn't hurt. Ask Tali."

Jay says, "That's all for now. You can step down." Jay says, "I call Tali Solace to the stand." Tali rises and walks over to the stand. After taking the oath of truth, she takes a seat.

Jay says, "Mrs. Solace. You've just heard Mr. Solace's description of your injuries resulting from the head-on collision with a wrong-way driver on the interstate. Please explain in your own words either confirming or denying his description of your injuries."

Tali says, "Mostly, his descriptions were pretty accurate. There were a few more injuries, but that's in the details and my X-rays."

"Okay, thank you for that confirmation," Jay says. "Let's go back to the evening at the restaurant where the police report states that Mr. Solace attacked you and pinned you against your car. Could you please either confirm or deny those events?"

"Yes," says Tali. "The police report is correct."

"Please state in your own words why you petitioned for divorce from Mr. Solace."

Tali looks intently at Jay and is careful not to look in Blake's direction, "I'm divorcing Blake for several reasons. Our marriage is irreparably broken. He's physically attacked me. We've heard some evidence of that. There have been other instances of physical abuse. The mental and emotional abuse that Blake has done to me—the daily rages and belittling—are obvious. My friends and family have been concerned about our marriage for quite some time. I finally got the courage to stand up to his bullying. I'm ready to end this façade of a relationship. I hope he finds what he's looking for."

Jay then says, "Mr. Solace admitted to a sexual encounter with you while you were trying to recover from your car wreck. Is that true?"

Tali says, "Yes. My hips were broken, my pelvis had been reinforced with metal plates, and my arms and legs were still bandaged from the previous surgeries. I couldn't stand or walk without assistance. He made me have sex that night, and I submitted. I was afraid not to. I was afraid if I didn't let him, he would get angry and hurt me in other ways. To this day, my Mamita, who was staying with us while I was recovering from the car wreck, still asks me why I didn't scream out that night. I was afraid. When he penetrated me with all of my injuries, the pain was awful." Tali tries to hold back the tears as she speaks.

Blake suddenly stands up and says, "She's lying! She wanted to make love to me that night! Don't believe her lies!"

The judge says, "Mr. Solace, sit down and be quiet, or you'll be in contempt of this court." He directs his next comment to Pamela: "Please control your client."

Jay sees Tali's distress and asks for a brief recess, which the judge approves.

Tali heads to the ladies' room, and Blake tries to catch up to her. Pamela heads him off. "Leave Tali alone." Blake storms off down the hallway toward the vending area. After about ten minutes, everyone returns to the courtroom.

Tali takes her place on the stand and Jay resumes his questioning. "Mrs. Solace, do you have any knowledge of Mr. Solace's offshore investments?"

"No. I do not," Tali says.

"So you didn't notice any differences in your joint bank account balances during your marriage to Mr. Solace?"

"No. I did not. But I have noticed Blake's additional spending recently. When I learned that he's been dating a lady named Hope, whom he met in Monterey, where he lives and works, the extra expenses made more sense. Other than that, I didn't notice other discrepancies. His colleague, Jeff, at his previous employer, told me something about investments that he and Blake were looking at once at a company picnic, but I didn't learn anything more about those investments from Blake."

Jay continues, "You kicked Blake in the parking lot of a restaurant twelve months ago?"

Tali answers, "Yes, I did, in self-defense. Blake pinned me against my car and wouldn't let me go. The police report contains the whole story."

"Why did you run out of the restaurant first, Mrs. Solace?"

Tali replies, "Blake threatened me when I said I wanted a divorce. I'd just questioned him about snooping in my art studio. I also told him I knew that he'd gone to New York, that it wasn't a business trip as he'd said, and that I knew he'd met with my best friend to convince him I was going mad. He didn't like being found out, and he got angry, so I decided to leave the restaurant. He followed me out to my car and pinned me against the window, pushing my face into the glass. At that moment, my memory returned about another night he attacked me in our home, when I woke up bleeding in the bathroom. He said I'd hit my head. I couldn't remember anything. As he was pushing my head against the car window, my whole memory of that previous attack came flooding back to me."

"Have you ever pressed any charges against Blake?"

"No. I don't want to punish him. I want a divorce. I'm not the right woman for him."

"Thank you, you're excused."

Pamela calls Blake's expert witness, a forensic accountant, to the stand. After he takes the oath, Pamela hands an exhibit to the forensic accountant and the judge. "Please explain what we're looking at in this spreadsheet and tell us if you're the expert who did these calculations."

He says, "Yes, I did the calculations in this spreadsheet. These calculations represent the expected cash flows from the marital assets Mr. and Mrs. Solace jointly own. On the second sheet, these are the calculations for the expected cash flows for Mrs. Solace upon completion of the divorce settlement."

Pamela says, "Interesting. Why does Mrs. Solace's projected payout dwindle to zero within the first twelve months after settlement?"

He replies, "Mr. Solace told me to calculate it that way. He says Mrs. Solace deserves nothing, but since we're in a community property state, he had to give her something in the first year."

Pamela continues, "I see the interest rate you used in the calculations stated at the top of the spreadsheet. How did you select that particular interest rate for your calculations?"

He replies, "Mr. Solace told me to use that interest rate in my calculations." The expert witness looks flustered. Pamela excuses the witness.

Jay stands as Pamela sits and calls Tali's expert witness, a forensic accountant, to the stand. After taking the oath of truth, Jay asks the witness to explain the spreadsheet containing expected cash flow calculations. The witness calmly and confidently explained the financial projections and calculations that she had provided. She added that she conducted multiple scenarios using relied-upon interest rates with reasonable outcomes for both Mr. and Mrs. Solace's fair division of the marital assets.

"Thank you. I'm finished with this witness." Jay asks Tali to return to the stand. "Do either you or Mr. Solace want to retain the townhouse?"

Tali replies, "Since Blake lives and works in Monterey, and I live and work in Newport Beach, I would like to buy out Blake's half of the townhouse. You said earlier that the judge would like us to sell the townhouse and split the profits. If necessary, I'll accept this with the stipulation that Blake will not direct the staging process. In my line of work, I have connections who can help us. I will do my best to preserve the townhouse's value to conclude the divorce settlement process."

Jay says, "We'll let the judge decide what to do with the townhouse then. That's all." Tali and Jay return to their seats.

The judge says, "Court is adjourned for today. Attorneys, meet me in my chambers in ten minutes."

Ten minutes later, Pamela and Jay are sitting in the judge's chambers while he reviews the exhibits and makes notes. After a few minutes pass, the judge says, "How in the world does someone like Blake Solace look at himself in the mirror each day with a clear conscience?"

"Only with a mask on, your honor," says Jay.

Pamela nods her head in agreement.

"Pamela, your client put on quite a show today. I almost called him on his obvious lies, but I decided to let him run with the bait a while, just for the entertainment value," the judge says.

"Thank you. I think I sweated through this new blazer today. Sweat equity, you know," Pamela says.

Jay chuckles. The judge says, "Okay then. Let's get this thing settled. Tali can buy out Blake's portion of the townhouse. You two figure out which appraisers to contact—at least three. Bring the appraisals back to me. Let's go with Tali's forensic accountant's calculations on projected cash flows for each party. Regarding Blake's potential offshore assets, I have an expert who can track those down for us. I'll call him when we're done talking here. What else? Each party keeps his or her car. Any questions?"

Jay and Pamela each thanked the judge for efficiently settling the case and exited the judge's chambers. The judge called his assistant to inquire about the contact information of the offshore investment expert. He expects the divorce decree should be ready for signatures within two weeks.

45

Enjoy the Journey

Tali walks out of the courthouse with a feeling of uncertainty. *How did that experience really go?* she wonders. She wants to talk with Jay. He said he'd call her tomorrow to follow up with the judge's instructions. He also told her not to worry. When she arrives at her car on the parking deck, she sits quietly, collecting her thoughts. Tears fill her eyes as she reflects on what was said in that courtroom today. So many emotions bubbled up. She silently calls out to God to help her gather some peace before she drives home, the home she hopes to retain after the divorce is finalized. If she can't, then she and the pets will make a new home somewhere else in Newport Beach.

Her phone buzzes again and again. First, Mamita, then Molly, and then Bentley are checking in on her. She feels so blessed to have friends and family who love her. When this divorce concludes, she has some reconnaissance to do on relationships that Blake tried to abort—especially rebuilding the relationship with her little brother Roman. *How could I have been so blind to Blake's evil antics? I miss Roman. I can't wait to see him next week.* Tali collects her thoughts and returns text messages before starting the engine. She lets everyone know she's okay and about to drive home. They each reply with a heart. She drives out of the deck and heads home. When she enters the townhouse, Jasper and Misty greet her happily. She bends down to hug and pet them both, then sits on the floor as they try to crawl into her lap. She starts to cry...not tears of pain...tears of joy. Misty purrs as Jasper licks the tears off her face. After a few moments, Tali rises and fills their water bowls. She goes upstairs to put on comfortable clothes and returns to get Jasper's leash. It's time to head out on their walk to the beach. The sun begins to set toward the horizon. Tali and Jasper walk casually. They have no reason to hurry. After about twenty minutes, Tali notices the outline of a figure in the distance. There is the appearance of an aura surrounding the image. A bit startled, Tali continues toward the figure, then she recognizes the face... Aaron.

Jasper runs ahead to greet Aaron, who kneels to pet her.

Aaron smiles as he greets Tali. "Hi. Do you remember me?"

She replies, "I do. You are Aaron. Jasper remembers you, too. What are you doing here?"

"Checking to see how you're doing."

"I'm fine. Did I do something wrong today?"

"No," he says, "nothing is wrong, Tali. God sent me. How are you?"

Tali says, "I feel uncertain about many things, but I'm relieved the court proceedings are over." She begins to cry and lets out all of her questions. "Why is Blake so mean? Why did I fall for him? What's going to happen to me? To my home? To my life? Will I ever know true love? I'm so confused. I'm sorry. I'm complaining too much."

Aaron gets up off the sand and walks over to her. He takes her hands and says, "Tali, you'll be okay. Do you realize that there's always been a plan for your life? For your decisions? Remember the bungee jumping?"

Tali giggles a bit as she looks up at him through her tears. "I guess," she replies. But I've wasted years of my life being with Blake."

"Not wasted," he says. "You're on a journey. You've learned valuable skills through this experience. You've learned from your conversations with Shannon. You and Jay expertly handled the courtroom adventure today. And aren't you trying to help LeeAnn with her relationship questions right now?"

Tali listens. "Well, yes. I suppose," she replies. "I just don't know how to figure out all the steps to get my life back in order when the divorce finalizes."

"You don't have to know, Tali. Let God lead you in your direction and decisions. He will. He has plans for you."

Tali looks at Aaron with doubt in her eyes. "If you say so. I know He does. I'm just worn out. Blake has worn me down to nothing. I'm so tired."

"It's okay. You'll get your energy and life back—Tali's new and improved version will take the world by storm! You'll see!"

Tali smiles and gives Aaron a big hug. "Thank you, Aaron. You're the best guardian angel ever; well, you're the only guardian angel I know." They both chuckle.

"You're welcome. You're going to be fine—better than fine. Are you and Jasper okay to walk back home now? There's still some light."

"Yes, we'll be fine. Thanks for looking out for us."

"Of course."

Tali looks down at Jasper for a few seconds, and when she looks up, Aaron is gone. She picks up Jasper's leash, and they start walking toward home. *Just enjoy the journey*, she thinks.

46

Caught in the Undertow

"Hi," she says, answering a call from Jay. "Any word on our court adventure?"

Jay replies. "Yes, there is. The judge decided to allow you to buy out Blake's half of the townhouse if you would still like to do that."

"Yes! So happy to hear that!" Tali exclaims. Jay continues, "The judge has commissioned financial experts to investigate offshore investments that we think Blake is hiding. The judge got an FBI agent to question one of Blake's former employees at the firm here in Newport Beach. He shared some information about Blake's investment schemes, including offshore accounts. I tell you what. Our judge is on fire to catch Blake in his lies. He told Pamela and me he purposely allowed Blake to run with the bait to see where Blake would take his lies. He found it to be quite entertaining."

Tali smiles and says, "I wouldn't call yesterday entertaining, but I trust that you legal types know what you're doing better than I do."

Jay chuckles. "Tali, I need you to review the judge's decision. I'm emailing you the draft. Blake is also receiving an email from Pamela. The judge will fill in the offshore investment details later today or tomorrow as soon as he hears back from his investigators. This case will wrap up soon."

"I hope so," says Tali. "It's been a grueling twelve months trying to divorce Blake. Severing the relationship with a narcissist is…" she pauses. "I don't know exactly how to categorize this experience…this journey. It's like being caught in an undertow at the beach. You know. Like you're drowning. But, I will say that having you as my attorney made this process as painless and seamless as possible."

"Thank you, Tali. You're definitely my most optimistic client. I will miss those sunny Sunday morning voicemails on my office phone after you've had all weekend to think about what Blake's been saying and doing and how we will handle it."

Tali laughs.

Jay continues, "Call me after you review the judge's recommendations, and then I'll contact Pamela to get Blake's comments. I can only imagine! We will discuss any disparity points. Hopefully, they will be small items. A narcissist must feel that they've 'won,' so maybe we can concede on something to help him feel like he's pushed the ball over the goal line. Sound like a plan?"

"Sure does," Tali says. "I'll review the draft and look forward to catching up later." They both say their goodbyes and end the call.

The next moment, Tali's phone buzzes with the crickets text tone. It's Blake.

He texts Tali. "You think you've won, but you haven't. There are a few things I plan to do to you. You're going to regret this."

Tali doesn't respond.

Blake texts again. "I'm here until tomorrow. The papers aren't signed yet. You can still call off this crazy divorce. I promise you'll be very sorry if you don't."

Tali doesn't respond. She screenshots Blake's texts and sends them to Jay. *Shannon tells me to keep neutral. Don't react to Blake's threats.* Troubled by the angry texts, she decides to continue ignoring him. She puts her phone aside and focuses on the positive call with Jay.

Later, she remembered she was going to follow up with Tia about some new looks for her café. Tia plans to add retail space to her café, and customers have asked her to write a cookbook sharing some of her spice combinations.

Tali has been experimenting with the art of repurposing, where broken ceramics are repaired with golden adhesive and then painted with liquid gold paint. The ceramics become artistic décor—no longer used for serving cuisine—but beautiful in their own way. Tali reflects on her injuries from the car wreck and how she continues to feel repurposed with her interior design adaptations to make spaces more accessible and beautiful for people using wheelchairs and gait aids. She's grateful her broken bones became stronger after healing.

"Let's see Tia this evening," she says to Jasper. "It will take my mind off Blake." Jasper is very willing.

Tia's Café is open late for the church group and anyone who wants to stop by for a lovely sunset, appetizers, drinks, and dinner.

Still a quarter mile down the beach from Tia's Café, Tali listens to the sounds of the waves and seagulls calling out. She hears a dull sound and feels a searing pain in her left shoulder as she falls to the sand. Jasper runs to her and licks her shoulder. Tali doesn't move.

Jasper runs up the beach to Tia's Café, barking the whole way. Tia goes to the window. Jasper runs inside the café, barking and running back toward the door.

"Jasper? Where's your mommy? You still have your leash on. What's happened?" Jasper keeps barking and circling back to the door.

"I get it!" Tia says and follows Jasper out the door. Jasper runs faster than Tia but keeps circling back so Tia will follow her. Tia squints her eyes as she looks toward the sunset on the horizon. Jasper runs toward something on the sand. Tia runs faster. As she nears the shoreline, she wonders if it is a dolphin, then sees it's a person. "Oh no! It's Tali!" she screams. Café patrons and a few wait staff had followed Tia and were close behind as she dropped to the sand. "Tali, are you okay?" No response. Tali's left shoulder is bleeding. She'd been shot. Tia touches Tali's neck and feels a light pulse, noticing her shallow breathing.

"Someone call 911!"

Her server, who was right behind her, says, "Already did. They're on the way."

Tia removes the scarf tied around her ponytail and holds it against Tali's bleeding shoulder. Jasper drops to the ground, breathing heavily but no longer barking.

The ambulance arrives, and paramedics run up the beach with equipment and a stretcher. They ask everyone to stand back as they measure Tali's vital signs and assess her injuries. She's unconscious.

Epilogue

Unconscious and wounded, Tali's battle to take control of her life takes on new dimensions. As police search for clues to identify the shooter, Tali must once again find the strength to heal not just from the bullet wound but the knowledge that someone tried to kill her. Her traumatized life just got much more complicated. Will the love of friends and family be enough to help her recover from yet another attack? Will her guardian angel be there for her? And what will surface in the investigation of her being shot? More turmoil. More churning. Tali believes that every gem must be polished with friction. How much more friction can she endure?

About the Author

Skye Bellarmine

Skye Bellarmine is an author who goes wherever the wind takes her. Her nomadic family was always moving, so she learned early to adapt to multiple environments and personality types. Skye's advanced studies have earned her a degree in life skills and her intuitive empathy has enabled her to learn from and rise above life's challenges. She doesn't take anything or anyone for granted and recognizes that the traumas in her life created her spirit, her spark, and her determination.

Breaking Solace is her first book. With the spirit of a brave warrior, her goal in writing is to help others gain the fortitude to stand up, stand out, and overcome abuse. Skye will help you ride the waves of life into a beautiful shore, teach you how to shine through the darkness and restart your life as many times as needed so that you can emerge as the gemstone you are meant to be.

https://starskyepress.com
email: skye@starskyepress.com

www.ingramcontent.com/pod-product-compliance
Lightning Source LLC
Chambersburg PA
CBHW061750120626
46550CB00005B/1952